To Amelie Belle, our new taster

First impression 2016
Second impression 2017

© Dylan and Llinos Rowlands, and Y Lolfa Cyf., 2016

Design: Richard Ceri Jones

ISBN: 978-1-78461-436-2

Printed and published and bound in Wales by Y Lolfa Cyf.,
Talybont, Ceredigion SY24 5HE.
e-mail ylolfa@ylolfa.com
website www.ylolfa.com
phone (01970) 832 304
fax 832 782

Rarebit & Rioja

Recipes and wine tales from Wales

DYLAN ROWLANDS · LLINOS ROWLANDS

y Lolfa

Rarebit & Rioja

Recipes and wine tales from Wales

Contents

 Preparation, not cooking, time.

Preface

What we choose to eat and drink is a personal thing, like music. Tastes vary, but once you've found a glass of wine or a song that makes you feel instantly at home, everything in the world seems alright. Much like those special songs we love, those warm nights, where a bottle or a meal is shared amongst friends, are made special, thanks to quality and the consistency of those who make them.

When it comes to this small, family-run restaurant settled deep in the stunning North Wales mountains, its quality, care and passion speaks for itself. Accolades adorn the walls, customers make pilgrimages here, and the care Dylan and Llinos show when importing these special wines from Spain, France, Austria and Italy, as well as prize-winning wines from Wales, is what makes Dylanwad such a special place. Using local food produce of the highest standards and prepared with care, creativity and an understanding that can only come with time, of what makes a meal delicious and memorable, there is little wonder that Dylanwad's story is one of fondness, family and new friends.

With Welsh tastes running through the venture, Dylanwad has proved itself to be as proud of Wales as Wales is of this family-run business. As this success story grows, so too does its physical home, marking a new era for this proud Welsh institution.

This book is a celebration of the story so far, and of the future and all that it holds. Stop, admire, and savour the moment, not too dissimilar to enjoying a glass of the good stuff.

Huw Stephens, BBC Radio DJ
January 2016

Introduction

How did I get here?

I was very fortunate to travel quite extensively with my family from an early age. Every year, Mum and Dad would pack the car to travel abroad from Essex for a fortnight to places that were, at the time, considered relatively exotic: France, Spain and Austria. This ignited in me a great interest in foreign countries and their diverse cultures and developed a somewhat eclectic palate when it came to food. Whilst I was still quite young, my parents bought a caravan; I often reminisce about these days with heartfelt sympathy for my poor father who drove along the pot-holed roads of Europe on a wing and a prayer all the way down to Yugoslavia in the 1960s. His experience as an air mechanic with the RAF during the Second World War stood him in good stead to cope with breakdowns and maintenance on the less reliable vehicles of the time. We all became adept at hitching and unhitching the caravan from the car in seconds to turn around when wrong turns had been taken on narrow roads. No sat-nav in those days.

My mother was a creative spirit and left me with a love for the arts and an equal passion for food. A talented calligrapher, she combined her skills to produce beautiful illustrated recipes. If my father was the holiday chauffeur then it's fair to say that Mum would shoulder the catering duties and the planning, packing all the necessary store-cupboard ingredients in every nook and cranny of the caravan, to be carted across Europe and sometimes back again! She relished the cooking on our trips, with the freshest of ingredients unavailable at home in those days, meals were a treat even produced from the tiny confines of the very basic kitchen. I hasten to add that there was a rota to ensure she had a break from the kitchen and this is when I produced my first ever menu. I hope that I have developed my skills somewhat since!

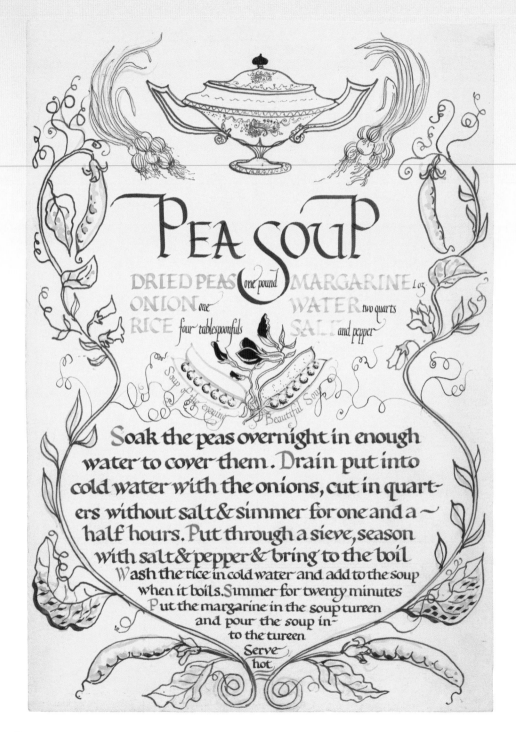

PEA SOUP

DRIED PEAS *one pound* MARGARINE *1 oz*
ONION *one* WATER *two quarts*
RICE *four tablespoonfuls* SALT *and pepper*

Soup of the evening *Beautiful Soup*

Soak the peas overnight in enough
water to cover them. Drain put into
cold water with the onions, cut in quarters without salt & simmer for one and a ~
half hours. Put through a sieve, season
with salt & pepper & bring to the boil
Wash the rice in cold water and add to the soup
when it boils. Simmer for twenty minutes
Put the margarine in the soup tureen
and pour the soup in-
to the tureen
Serve
hot

So I caught the travelling bug and had the confidence to venture off on my own during the 1980s after graduating from Exeter University. My first major trip began in Houston, USA, courtesy of Freddie Laker and I weaved my way right down to Argentina, enjoying the different foods available in Central and South America. It had quite an impact upon me and the warmth of welcome to a lonely traveller went a long way. Seeing the pleasure it was possible to create in a cafe, roadside stand or in a formal restaurant was my epiphany in many ways. People have memorable meals, and mine was on a small back street in Cuzco, Peru. Women gathered early evening to sell food out of buckets which they would ladle onto plates that probably just passed for clean after a quick swill in another bucket that served as a dishwasher. Potato and meat stew for pennies served by a jolly crew of women who were so friendly and warm: it tasted so good – I'll never forget it.

During the early 1980s recession it was tough trying to find a job, but as usual, the catering industry always had something to offer and I started as a kitchen assistant in a hotel in Fairbourne. This served as a springboard for other jobs and I moved from one place to the other; each contributing to my skills set in different ways. I was enjoying myself!

Within a relatively short time, I had moved to something totally different – nominally the Head Chef (in a team of one!) at a country house hotel, Abergwynant Hall, before moving on to buying my own restaurant. A small bistro in Dolgellau called La Petite Auberge, owned by Evelyn and Yannick Tonnerre and Georges Dewez came on the market and this was too good to ignore. Evelyn and Yannick wanted to return to France and on the 31st July 1988, we moved in. On the 2nd August, we were open for the first night of running my own restaurant.

Following the first winter, the time came to put my own stamp on the place. Dolgellau is a close-knit Welsh community and I wanted to be a part of the fabric and make my own contribution to the economy and culture so the name was important. We held a competition and a

One of the best jobs was cooking fish and chips in Pat Nunn's café.

9

*The early days
were very hard
and we were
extremely busy.*

talented writer and friend, Sue Roberts from Trawsfynydd came up with Dylanwad Da. This translates to 'Good Influence' whilst incorporating my name, Dylan. It has served us well over the years and as we leaned more towards the wine trade, we developed it to 'Dan y Dylanwad' (Under the Influence) for that side of the business. It hopefully conveyed in part some of our values: to support a local community whilst reaching out to the wider world and draw in new experiences for the locality. Friends recently described Dolgellau as a 'microcosm and a little hub that collects and pulls in other influences' and I like the thought of this. It is a refuge, we are safe here and we need to look after and preserve our culture and language but it is also important to prospect: survey the world and gather, in order to bring back and enrich. It's a fine balance of preservation and development.

The step from being a chef to running your own business is a huge one; you are responsible for a great deal more than just preparing food, and selecting wines for our list with little experience was definitely new to us. So I'm sure the name partly influenced our choice of an early house wine: Rowlands Brook. It was good but I hope my selection skills have developed since then and go beyond enjoying the name.

I think an early influence with wine is thanks to Georges, who for a short time lived upstairs with us whilst waiting to buy his new home. He was a great fisherman and what a delight it was, seeing him return from a fishing trip with

twelve suitably-sized Grayling laid out immaculately in the boot of his car for me to put on the menu. He also showed me the best place to pick the delicious Chanterelle mushrooms from local woods. Occasionally, he would visit Chester or another nearby city for the day and at the end of service, we would hear him padding down the stairs with a special cheese and a bottle of sherry or red wine to sit and enjoy whilst chatting round the little table in the kitchen. I have a lot to thank him for. In return, we provided him with a partner – my wife Llinos' friend, Jane, used to visit and eventually we noticed she was visiting another resident in our household rather than us!

Running a small restaurant like Dylanwad Da is never going to make you wealthy but it pays other dividends and I think it is safe to say that our lives have been enriched by all of the friends we have made: customers and definitely staff. Some of the staff, like Emma, probably feel as though they have been here for longer than me and sometimes seem to know me better than myself. We're still in touch with most of our staff, many who have long since left the area but we keep in touch and meet up and many have become close friends. It's satisfying to feel we have kindled an interest in food and wine in staff and we certainly see them regularly in our new premises, sampling from the pods and our annual (informal) lunch club stands testament to this. We've eaten at some of the best establishments together. One of the enduring memories I have is of sitting on a bench at the Royal Chelsea Hospital gardens with Wendy, Lowri, Karen and Emma, slugging cheap Cava from plastic cups before lunch at Gordon Ramsay's – sorry, Gordon!

Naturally, I suppose, our two sons, Tom and Meirion, have a strong interest in food and drink too. After the complaints about school meals barely managing to fill a corner of the stomachs of two growing teenage boys approaching 6ft in height, I began to cook lunches for them and soon their friends too. In the run up to Christmas, lunches were immensely popular, often drawing a gang of them down during break from school to hoover up the leftovers from the many turkey dinners. By now, the two cook regularly and Tom has also completed a couple of wine courses.

It took years to build up the business and put our own stamp on it and throughout this time our interest in wine developed from a heavy dependence on one supplier and little knowledge to inform our decisions, to increasing confidence to select from different wholesalers, and eventually importing our own and securing real control and value for money for our customers.

One defining moment about 20 years ago came after one of our parties (we used to have quite a few in our younger days!). Llinos was clearing out the bottles when she called me over to have a look at the empties and the range of countries was striking, showing a move from France and Germany with possibly the odd Chianti or Rioja, to countries such as Chile, New Zealand and Australia.

The only way to learn is by tasting, and we did a lot of that in the early days.

In 1998 the time came for me to fill in some of the gaps in my knowledge with a formal wine course and along with my friend Mark from Penmaenuchaf Hall Hotel, I registered for a course in Newtown. It was some journey for the two of us but we shared the driving so that each of us could taste properly on alternate weeks. The 'bug' had truly bitten by now and the following year found us travelling to Colwyn Bay for the next level of training. The trouble is, the more you learn, the more you realise how much you don't know about this vast and fascinating subject and the obsession then culminated in the WSET Diploma. This took two years of travelling from North Wales to London and my wife regularly reminds me of the time I returned after the first year exams, head in hands, declaring it was the worst day of my life. And it really was, worse than my university finals, much worse, because this time I suppose, I cared. There aren't many comparable experiences to sitting in a hot sweaty room in West London nervously trying to identify six different wines presented to you blind.

However, this gave me the confidence to press on to look for wines to import directly and so my travels took me to Turin, Italy before moving on soon after to Spain, France and Austria. This was perfect, it gave me the opportunity to combine my love of travelling, food and wine. They say that you should find something you love doing and then find a way of getting paid to do it, and that's precisely what I intend to do! Every time I go away, I make a point of booking a table in a good restaurant at least one of the nights. I don't mind staying in a relatively cheap hotel, I'm not fussy and I like a bargain, but I will not compromise on my food and wine.

By now, the restaurant is an important part of my history but we have moved on again, with the help of the fantastic LEAD business leadership course in Bangor and especially my mentor. Sue Heatherington, who took me on some very insightful journeys of analysis of the business and myself. We have gone into the wine trade full time with our new shop and wine bar while wholesaling to others. I was proud of what we achieved in Dylanwad Da and now I hope that we can be equally proud of what we will achieve in our specially renovated 17th century building in Dolgellau: to offer locals and visitors the opportunity to taste and enjoy good wines from around the world in a modern and comfortable environment.

We are grateful to Y Lolfa for having faith in the book in both Welsh and English. We would also like to thank friends, staff, family and customers – especially the loyal people of Dolgellau and the surrounding area, who have supported us for nearly 30 years now. We are also very grateful to individuals for the testing recipes: Hayley Evans, Sandie Williams (we'll never forget your version of the rarebit!) and Jannet Lawley. Thanks to Tom Black for allowing us to use his research on Ancre Hill. Finally, special gratitude to Tom Griffiths who took many of the photographs including the front and back cover, Andy Jones for the photo of Gwin Dylanwad Wine, and Elin Hughes for her lovely little illustrations.

Dylan & Llinos Rowlands
January 2016

Producing wine

A Welsh vocabulary for wine

With increasing frequency, I conduct wine tastings in venues from village halls in rural villages to corporate events in Cardiff. I enjoy these events and see it as a part of the business and have been more than comfortable conducting these in English. It was initially trickier in Welsh, but again, I enjoy this experience and it helps me to develop my own language. This did however pose a problem in that there was an absence of wine vocabulary in Welsh. I found it a challenge to fill this void during tastings. We are used to talking about 'oak in a wine' or 'a delicate and floral nose' in English but this is relatively new, along with people's growing interest in wine. You only have to cast your mind back to the sometimes outrageous descriptions offered by Gilly Goolden on the early TV programme when wine knowledge within the general public was in its infancy.

So, slowly, I'm accumulating a vocabulary in Welsh. Context is everything, therefore the word needs to sit comfortably and usage breeds familiarity where it may have sounded odd at one time. We need this vocabulary to describe the primary characteristics of what we are tasting – labels to remind us of our experience of smell and taste, in order that we may recall them when we next taste the same grape or for comparison with others. Whilst the words sometimes seem a bit strange at first in Welsh (you hear people talk of a 'good mousse' to describe the froth on a poured glass of sparkling and this was strange to the English ear at one time). Similarly, the 'bead' is the fine little line of bubbles snaking its way up the glass of a sparkling wine, and we decided after several discussions that the word 'mwclis' in Welsh (necklace) was more appropriate and prettier! So it's an interesting and creative process and we shall see if any develop into general use. Anyway, here's a list (not definitive) for your interest and for any learners who want to broach the subject.

Gwinaeaf 1.	Vintage
Eplesiad	Fermentation
Eplesu	Ferment
Gwinllan	Vineyard
Gwinwr/wraig	Wine maker
Gwinwyddaeth	Viticulture
Gwneud gwin	Vinification
Gwaddod	Sediment
Grawnwin	Grape
Gwinwydden	Vine
Gwinwydd	Vines
Blodeuog	Floral
Ffrwythus	Fruity
Canolig	Medium-bodied
Llawn	Full-bodied
Ysgafn	Light
Casgen	Barrel
Dur gwrthstaen	Stainless steel
Tanin	Tannin
Ardywallt	Decant
Decanter	Decanter
Llymaid	Sip
Glaswelltog	Grassy
Perlysiau	Herbs
Licris	Liquorice
Llysieuol	Vegetal
Troelli	Swirl
Corcio (wedi)	Corked (tainted)
Arogl	Nose
Golwg	Appearance
Blas	Taste
Byrlymus/Pefriog	Sparkling
Bwrlwm	Fizz
Mŵs	Mousse
Mwclis	Bead
Hyd	Length

1. This is a word that was created in a Twitter discussion with 'Gwyddeles', who actually lives in Asturias, Spain. What a sociable business this is!

Developing an interest in wine

During the last 25 years there has been a huge increase in the public's interest in wine. Starting my restaurant business in 1988, there was very little choice outside the traditional European market, and this meant France, Italy, Spain and Germany on the whole. People weren't familiar with grape varieties and very little interest was shown in choosing much beyond the house wine. It's a very different world now, with a desire to learn about wine and increasingly sophisticated taste-buds wanting more knowledge about what they are drinking and demanding quality and variety. The pleasure of discovering the story behind the bottle is infectious, with locals and visitors alike eager to learn about the different aspects from geography, geology, science before we even begin to talk about the cultural aspects that affect and are attached to the production of wines. This was highlighted for me recently when I visited yet another new Welsh vineyard called Llaethliw. Intrigued by the seafaring theme on the label with a cutter bobbing on waves, I was delighted to discover a historical reason for this dating back to the 19th century owner of the farm's share in the ship and its cargo. The more I discover, the more I want to learn.

Talking of farms, I remember my wife's first visit with me to a vineyard in the Loire valley. Though a vast field, I think sometimes we need to demystify the wine-making process, and this is precisely what she did. As we trod through the vineyard following the winemaker in his boiler suit and wellies he bemoaned the fact that the weather had been unfavourable and shook his head as he lifted a cluster of mouldy grapes for us to see. On our return to the car, Llinos said, 'Actually, they're farmers, just like my dad'. This is so true and though stating the obvious, it was a bit of a revelation. I think we need to remember that the majority of producers are not wealthy, grand *châteaux* owners but workers of the land, developing a product of the land with all of the difficulties that any farmer or gardener faces in the variable and unpredictable natural world. It is these small producers that I am interested in

The pleasure of discovering the story behind the bottle is infectious

The product and its quality is dependent on nature and the grower.

buying wine from. By building relationships with these people over the years, I have developed a better understanding and appreciation of the six factors that contribute to the wine-making process. These are essential to the taste and quality of what we all enjoy drinking and a quick breakdown of these is what follows.

If you have ever grown your own vegetables or fruit you'll be aware of a number of these factors, and growing grapes is no exception. Remember, you can only make great wine with great grapes, the best you can get from your *terroir*.

Soil

The kind of soil you have affects what grows out of it: there may be more chalk in the land or it may be granite; more, or less, iron can make a difference to the flavour of the grape and may suit certain varieties better than others.

Sometimes it's hard to comprehend how a few paces from one field to the next can make a marked difference in the quality – and the price. If you ever travel through Burgundy, take the D974 Route des Grandes Crus, you will see that virtually all of the vineyards are on the slopes to your left as you head north, with maize and other crops to the right. One after another you see the names of world famous villages such as Volnay, Meursault and Montrachet and you can see the effect of the *terroir*. If you study more closely you will see precisely where the very best vineyards are within these areas, the differentiating factor being the soil, as the grapes are all Chardonnay or Pinot Noir. The best sites tend to be in the mid slope, where the soil and aspect is perfect for making the very best wines.

However, it is not necessarily good quality soil that is required, see the picture of the *galets* in Chateauneuf – rocks that would look more at home on Fairbourne beach – and the vines grow out from these, forcing the roots deep down to gather micro amounts of minerals and nutrients from the soil.

Climate

Once again, just like the soil, any farmer or gardener knows how dependent they are on the climate, and grapes prosper with a good temperate climate to grow in: not too hot or cold, too dry or wet and with proper seasons. Britain is right on the margin of where it is possible to grow grapes well and this area extends right down to Morocco and Tunisia in the south but here it gets too hot and arid. This is more than likely going to be the problem facing some wine-growing regions in Australia in the southern hemisphere where the increasing temperature is almost on the border of being too hot for wine production.

Weather

What you choose to do or not to do will have an effect on the wine.

As opposed to climate, the weather changes from year to year, and that's why knowing the vintage of a wine is more important in areas such as Burgundy and Bordeaux but not for Australia where the weather is more consistent. This becomes even more of a factor in our own country, Wales, where the weather is variable from year to year and of course, the vines will grow better with a bit more sun and a little less rain especially at the end of the growing season. An example of the British winegrower's susceptibility to the weather was seen in the 'memorable' cold, wet vintage of 2012, when one of Britain's top sparkling producers decided not to harvest their grapes – an extremely brave and difficult decision and one of the disadvantages of being such a northerly grower.

Viticulture

This is where human intervention truly begins to have its effect, the care and treatment of the plant can make a great difference and the winemaker has several choices. One is how to prune, controlling the growth and deciding how many bunches each vine will produce. You will notice that in some countries the vines are grown high above the cold earth or elsewhere low to benefit from the warm soil at night. What you choose to do or not to do will have an effect, as well as the decision whether to irrigate or not (of course, in Europe, they may not irrigate in the quality wine areas unless exceptional circumstances prevail, and there are strict rules regarding how this is done). Some winemakers will choose to remove leaves to improve the exposure to the sun for their grapes. Others will remove clusters of grapes before they ripen to concentrate the flavours in fewer bunches – a smaller harvest but better quality, they hope.

Vinification

There is no magic involved in the winemaking process. If you place bunches of grapes in a bucket, break them up somewhat and leave them somewhere warm they will begins to ferment and turn into wine. However, to make an acceptable drink there are many decisions to be made by the winemaker from the beginning. When to harvest the grapes? What to put them in: stainless steel or wooden barrels? The fermentation temperature. What to age the wine in – tanks, barrels or bottles? In the limited space I have here, there is no room to do full justice with such a vast subject but already we can see the layered effect of nature and human intervention that contributes to the process of transforming grapes to wine.

Grape variety

Whereas 25 years ago there was limited knowledge about grape varieties there is now a revolution in the general public's interest and knowledge about the subject and most people are now familiar with the classic grape varieties. Sauvignon, Chardonnay, Riesling, Cabernet Sauvignon, Syrah and Pinot Noir dominate but other lesser-known varieties are becoming well-known and taking their place on the shelves to become a part of the wine drinker's regular parlance. Just like apples, there is a unique taste to each variety. We know that Granny Smiths are different to Russets or Golden Delicious, well, there are at least 1,000 different varieties of grapes used to make wine worldwide. We are still attached to the most popular but I am pleased to see that our discerning customers are becoming more adventurous and finding the pleasure of tasting interesting grapes such as Grüner Veltliner from Austria, Arneis from Piedmonte or even Areni Noir from Armenia.

Tasting wine

Ok, so what about the wine-tasting process? Pure snobbery and nonsense that struggles to find a scientific justification? Much fun has been made (not least in my own home I have to say!) of the sometimes flamboyant and excessive descriptions associated with the wine-tasting world. Maybe they are absurd at times but I would like to make a case for the credibility of a wine-tasting vocabulary and recognise its merit as an essential part of a specialist subject that provides a scaffold to becoming a better-informed and more selective buyer. This is in addition to being one of the most pleasurable pastimes, enveloping geography, science and culture in a glass.

Take your passion for wine seriously. If you pay careful attention to your tasting and your personal labelling of tastes and aromas, you will know what to look for next time. Here are some small steps that can be of help to anyone who is new to the process when choosing from the shelves. This will help you to recognize the main characteristics that attract you to a wine or a particular taste. Remember that it's your own taste and preferences that are important.

The glass

Choose a wine glass with a nice wide bowl that narrows at the mouth. This means you can swirl the wine, and the aromas will be held in the glass so you can appreciate them properly. Personally, in the shop, I use specialist tasting glasses that are ISO standard and I use these for tastings too. You may have heard of some companies that produce specialist glasses to match the grapes, so you would have a particular glass for a Chardonnay and a different one for Shiraz, let's say. Now I know this may sound a bit extreme, but I have been to tastings using these glasses and believe it or not, it can make a significant

difference. However, we shall stick with our ordinary glasses for now and move methodically through the stages of wine-tasting.

Appearance

If it is cloudy there is more than likely a problem.

Pour about 2 to 3cm of wine into the glass, no more, in order for you to be able to swirl it without soaking your friends. The first thing you need to do is observe the colour; you will gain information about the wine immediately before even tasting it. If it is cloudy there is more than likely a problem, unless you know that this is a characteristic of that particular wine. If it has a bit of age, it may be that the sediment has been disturbed and combined with the wine, in which case it needed decanting.

The colour of a wine can tell you a great deal about the age of a wine or beginning the process of identifying a grape variety. It is not a hard and fast rule, but often the colour of a white wine becomes darker to a deep golden yellow with age or when it has been in oak barrels. Red wine on the other hand shows its age by transforming from a bright purple through to red mahogany before turning brick-red. Using a white background, turn your glass to study the edge of the wine which may appear to be breaking up slightly and have a rather watery quality on the rim if it is an ageing red.

Next, note the colour, for example, clear, yellow, dark purple, light red? Can you see through the glass when you look down at the stem or is it a solid block of colour? If it is a transparent red it could lead you to initial thoughts that it is more likely a Pinot Noir rather than a dark Syrah. You can see how it is a process of elimination as well as one of identification. As you proceed through each step, this vast subject narrows a little each time – well, that's the hope anyway!

By looking at the glass you can see, to some degree, the signs of strong alcoholic content by observing the 'tears' or 'legs' that run down the side of the glass after giving it a

swirl. If they are numerous and long it can be a sign that the alcohol content is high but this must be coupled with the tasting process. I am sure you have sometimes noticed a red sheen or coating left on the glass and this is due to high extraction and can be an indication of possibly being produced in a hot climate.

Aroma

Naming, or labelling, a smell is quite an art and it takes a lot of practice. You will often hear of fruits, herbs, grassy, cigar box, vegetal descriptions or maybe 'Cat's pee on a gooseberry bush' – Jancis Robinson's famous description of a New Zealand Sauvignon! (I promise to steer clear of animal or bodily fluids in my adjectival choices.) Personally, I do try to raise my 'smell awareness' as often as I can by paying attention to the aromas of fruits, chocolate and herbs when I come across them. This creates a word bank of aromas ready for the identification process when tasting. It really is a bit like learning a new language, and repetition is important. It is also fine to have your own words – it is whatever it is to you and the more you practise, the easier it becomes.

Swirl the wine in the glass to allow the aromas to fill the bowl of the glass and then take a good deep sniff. You can repeat this, but not more than a couple of times because your senses become accustomed to the smell very quickly. It doesn't take long but concentrate for that time, maybe ten seconds, to go through this process and come to a decision. This is the second stage where you can note faults with the wine. If it smells musty there is good chance that it is corked. This is a taint that is caused by a disease in the cork itself and has been greatly reduced in the last 10 years by the use of stelvin closures (screwcap), plastic corks and better quality corks.

Try to name what becomes immediately apparent: dark fruits, tropical fruits or possibly liquorice or herbs. Your first impressions are what count, you can savour it later but I find long deliberation initially doesn't add much more to your notes!

Taste

'About time' I hear you say, but the pleasure, as well as the identification process involves all of the senses and whilst the taste is important you need the aromas of the wine to circulate around your mouth and to your olfactory tract. This is possibly the stage that people find most bizarre – the gurgling sound tasters sometimes make as they draw air through the wine while it is in their mouths. This is in order to experience the full flavour by using your sense of smell at the same time. This is a bit like reversing the whistling process and creates a boiling sensation in your mouth as you swirl it around a couple of times. As long as you don't choke at this stage, I think you will be surprised at the increased tasting sensation you experience by doing this. At this point, when tasting professionally, you spit out the wine to preserve sobriety and judgement but this does not necessarily mean you are stone cold sober as I discovered a few years ago.

During a tasting in London, a friend had brought along a breathalyser for interest's sake. Even though I had tasted over forty wines, I knew I had not swallowed a drop, for two reasons: I wanted to be able to concentrate on the wines but more importantly, I had to drive home to Dolgellau from Welshpool train station that night. I huffed and I puffed and to my dismay, at Euston, I was over the legal limit to drive! I had absorbed the equivalent to a couple of glasses of wine or more through my tongue and mouth and into my bloodstream. What a lesson! By Shrewsbury the device showed amber, and luckily by the time I finally reached my car I was safe to drive.

Anyway, back to the tasting, and once again, practising and attempting to recall the words that label tastes for you is important. The way a wine can feel in your mouth is different, from one big hit of fruit that leaves you relatively quickly to something that has a more layered depth. 'Body' is often a word used to describe wine – light, medium or full, the 'mouthfeel'. I've heard it explained as like the difference in feel between water and milk in the mouth.

It's worth mentioning oak at this point and, again, this is a field to which I could devote an entire and rather lengthy chapter. Don't worry, I won't. I shall restrict myself to a few points in this book. Firstly, the taste of oak in the best wine comes from the best barrels whether they are made out of oak from France, America or wherever and they do taste different! In the cheaper wines they may achieve the oaked taste by using oak chips that are immersed in the wine in what can be best described as a giant teabag.

With better wines, you are looking for extra aromas and flavours for complexity.

Finally, when you taste wine and we talk about 'length', it is to convey the duration of the taste left in your mouth. A good quality wine should have good length that you can savour and enjoy.

Conclusion

You have to make a judgement about the wine finally, and the most important question is have you enjoyed it? If so, which characteristics did you like most so that you can remember them the next time? It does add to the fun to have a blind tasting so that you can try and guess some things when tasting. It also forces you to concentrate. Start with which grape or country or more significantly, the quality and price. Give it a go!

Decanting

When a wine ages, especially red, sediment can gather at the bottom of the bottle and this can be as fine as powder, creating a sludge in the bottom of the bottle and threatening to ruin a good wine if it mixes with the contents. Don't confuse this with the crystals you sometimes see in young bottles. These are perfectly harmless and they will not affect the wine. There is a general belief that decanting any bottle of wine, particularly young reds, helps it to open out. I don't know if this is true, but it certainly won't do any harm.

It's a simple process. With an old bottle, stand it upright for 24 hours for the sediment to settle. These wines should previously be kept in a rack with the label facing upwards so the sediment isn't hidden, and when the time comes to move them, do so very carefully in order that you don't stir the sediment too much. You need a good light and a decanter or a jug – any vessel is fine as long as it's clean. You may wash the bottle clean of the sediment in order to pour the wine back in if you wish, or pour it from the decanter or jug. Remove the cork with as little movement as you can manage, then hold the bottle above the light to gently pour into the decanter. Keep an eye on the sediment so that it stays in the bottom of the bottle and doesn't mix with the wine. With a good light you will see it start to head to the neck of the bottle near the end – stop before it mixes with the wine in your decanter. I know it goes against the grain, especially with an expensive bottle, but it is inevitable that you will have to waste a little of the wine in the bottom of the bottle – it is undrinkable. And there you have it. The wine is ready to drink.

Wine tips

- Don't overchill wines, it kills the taste (unless you want to kill the taste of a cheap and disappointing wine!).
- Store your wine in a room where the temperature is constant.
- The kitchen is one of the worst places to store your wine: too hot and fluctuating temperature.
- Store wine on its side to prevent the cork drying out.
- Don't throw leftover wine. It will keep for at least a month for cooking purposes.
- Shiraz is the New World name for the Syrah grape.
- When a wine is described as 'corked' it means there is a taint from the cork that has affected the wine, leaving a bad taste and aroma.

Italy

After passing my WSET (Wine and Spirit Education Trust) diploma in London, I decided the time had come to bite the bullet and actually start importing my own wine as an additional facet to the restaurant business. With the vast array of Italian wines to research I had to start somewhere. Luckily, cheap and convenient flights to most of Europe were numerous and I was soon on my way to Turin to attend my first wine show. It was a huge event, with wines from the four corners of Italy, ready to taste and buy. I decided to focus on Piedmonte, the region around Turin, but even after restricting myself to one area there was still a plethora of wines to choose from. All day I tasted. How to arrive at a decision? I was so new to all of this. Nevertheless, I trusted my instinct: the wines I had tasted during the morning remained in my memory. The quality was there and in addition to that, the striking and beautiful labels lovingly designed by the winemaker had impressed me. Let's be honest, we can all be influenced by the look of the bottle. Before leaving, I ventured back to the stall where Vincenzo's English-speaking friend had arrived and facilitated the negotiations greatly. Within a month, along with Maria, an old university friend to act as translator and my Dad as chief photographer, I was back on a plane destined for Turin – just for a day this time and on flights that only cost a penny each! We hired a car at the airport and it was only a short drive to Cisterna d'Asti, a tiny little village perched prettily on a hill.

Sitting in Vincenzo and Giovanna's beautiful and homely kitchen by the shiny ceramic stove, we tasted again. It confirmed the high standard of the wine and I was certain that this family would provide my first import to Dolgellau. Our business relationship continues to this day with this lovely family. Cristina, their daughter is studying wine at university and has learnt excellent English to ease communication and so the next generation is there to secure the future of the vineyard.

Prosecco

I had terrible difficulties during my first visit to Valdobbiadene. We're now harking back to the days when I was stubbornly refusing to own a mobile phone. Following this episode, our son Meirion bought one for my 50th to end my Luddite stand against the growing tide of technology. Back to Italy, I was on a research trip (I love this job!) and had chosen a hotel right in the middle of the area: the owner had asked me to call him when I arrived in the square in Valdobbiadene, so I borrowed a friend's mobile to make life easy.

On arrival, I sat in my car swearing at the phone as darkness descended. Finally, I gave up the battle and resorted to the tried and tested method of making contact: go to a bar, pay for a drink to obtain loose change and use a decent old-fashioned landline. Then I had to wait – in the bar of course – for the owner to come and guide me along the snake-like roads that criss-crossed on the vineyard slopes. This is the heart of Valdobbiadene and Conegliano where the best Prosecco is produced – better than the flat lands that extend towards Venice. It is a sparkling wine that has fresh grapey aroma made using a different method to Champagne, usually with a touch of sweetness. It is freshly produced throughout the year and should be drunk young, not one to be kept in the cellar for too long. The popularity of Prosecco increased with the famous Bellini cocktail from Harry's Bar in Venice, made by placing a dessertspoon of peach purée in the bottom of a Champagne flute before adding Prosecco. Simple! Give it a try!

The next morning, after the late night arrival and all the worrying, I awoke to look out of my window at vines stretching across the hills. I ventured out for a quick walk to get the lie of the land before my first appointment when I spotted something odd in the landscape. Amongst the vineyards, there were huge metal, funnel-shaped objects pointing to the sky like trumpets. On enquiring, I was told that they were hail cannons. Hail can cause devastating damage to vines and these cannons are used to ignite acetylene and oxygen. The shockwave that is caused by the explosion travels through the clouds at the speed of sound and, in theory, stops hail forming thus forcing it to fall as rain. Interesting! I don't know if it works but it was fun hearing the story.

Mistaken identity

What would they have thought of my tiny kitchen in North Wales in comparison to their glazed state of the art chef's lab!

One of my extravagances when in a foreign country is to book a special meal, therefore I booked my table in advance by e-mail in a Michelin-starred establishment. I was a bit doubtful having not had a confirmation and sure enough, when I arrived half an hour early, they were closed and what's more, hadn't received my e-mail. Fair play, they made no fuss and had a table ready for me in a matter of minutes. I was amused to see *tendon* on the menu and assumed it was a translation error for 'tenderloin' but no, it was tendon, the waitress indicated to the back of her knee: 'Tendon, speciality of the area,' she explained. Well, when in Rome... It was an interesting salad but perhaps not something we'll be serving in the future.

It is not unusual for me to be writing notes when out for a special meal. I am usually alone, and it is a time to catch up or revise what I have written during the day. It's a chance to mull over the wines I've tasted and meditate about the decision as to whether or not to import. This is precisely what I was doing when I noticed a face staring at me through the window in the kitchen door. I was feeling a little disconcerted when another face appeared, and then a third. It suddenly dawned on me that the service had been extra special with little finishing touches, such as the gold leaf with the first course being brought to my attention.

They had mistaken me for a Michelin inspector. I don't know whether they felt relief or disappointment.

The Bortolin Angelo family

One of the wines I was deliberating about that night was the Prosecco from Bortolin Angelo – a modern, clean winery owned by a family with a clear vision for their business: solar panels on the roof go hand in hand with sustaining old traditions. The business is in the careful hands of Desiderio and his sister Paola, the third generation of guardians of the vineyard established by their grandfather, and still producing the same type of wine with the same variety of grapes. This was the best quality and offered value for money. I could also see the love and respect with which they treated their wines. This was definitely the one for me – and I still import from them to this day.

Aperitifs

I have mentioned sparkling wines with canapés but there are many other aperitifs of course. In France, it is traditional to drink Kir: one small measure of the blackcurrant liqueur Crème de Cassis in the glass, topped up with white wine. Better still, top it up with Champagne or another sparkling wine to make a Kir Royale. Try giving it a Welsh twist by using the Aerona liqueur from Pen Llŷn, or the Italian favourite Bellini of Prosecco and peach purée.

Personally, I like a glass of sherry. All sherry is made from the white Palomino grape in the Jerez area of south-west Spain, with the help of Pedro Ximénez to vary the sweetness levels. The name is an English adaption of the town name, Jerez, and British families and traders have played an essential part in the development of fortified wines such as Sherry, Marsala, Port and Madeira.

There are so many sherries available, varying in sweetness as well as the way they are made. In my opinion, the dry ones make the best aperitifs such as the Fino, and my personal choice again would be the Manzanilla, which comes from the seaside town of Sanlúcar de Barrameda. There's a slightly salty taste to it. Once, in Sanlúcar, I was visiting one of the bodegas and whilst having a little lunchtime sniffter in one of the lovely plazas I noticed about twenty office workers sitting at a long table loaded with seafood. What drew my attention even more was the row of Manzanilla bottles in ice that was served with the food. It was a revelation and though it isn't a custom in Britain I did, during my years as a chef, occasionally serve sherry as a match for food and it was quite popular. I can't help but think lunchtimes like that create happier workforces!

Canapés and Tapas

Canapés and tapas are different animals but you can just adjust the portion size and both are interchangeable to some degree. Spaniards can be seen enjoying tapas with their drinks, even though free tapa with a drink is becoming a rarity these days. You need to leave the popular tourist traps to see this custom now. What a pleasure it is to sit with a glass of wine and have a small bowl of almonds or some *boquerones* (anchovies) on a slice of bread or something a bit more substantial such as *tortilla*, *patatas bravas* or *albóndigas* (meatballs). Travel north to the Basque country and you discover a different kind of tapas: pinchos. The beautiful town of Donostía (San Sebastián) has a myriad of bars in the squares and narrow streets of the old town. Early evening, it is a treat to see the counters resplendent with their offerings for the lively and noisy customers that pack the area. Further west, and a bit cheaper, the town of Bilbao offers excellent pinchos, as well as the famous and beautiful Guggenheim museum. It is fun to wander the streets until the early hours trying the wines and the pinchos, and watching people enjoying themselves.

Little nibbles of tasty food with a glass of your favourite tipple is an excellent way of provoking an appetite, so for canapés, choose something light that won't fill your guests. About three or four pieces each should be enough. The whole point is that they should be easy and flavoursome. I hate a battle with a canapé that is just too large to fit in my mouth or a topping that has been placed on a base that is insubstantial. Make them small and place them on a firm but not tooth-cracking base. Choose one that matches the food: blinis, toast, oatmeal biscuits are some of the best or mini choux buns. Use a small pastry cutter to produce tiny little circles onto which you can neatly place the food. For a tapas evening, choose something more substantial, possibly meat-based, that is easy to prepare before hand. The meatballs are a good option for this.

The popularity of a bit of fizz before a meal or with canapés is undeniable. There are several on the market and it is produced in a variety of ways. Champagne is made by first making a base wine in the usual way, and then it is subjected to a second fermentation in the bottle, adding some more sugar and yeast to the wine before closing the bottle with a crown top. The CO2 that is released during the second fermentation is trapped in the bottle to create the beautiful bubbles. This is the *méthode champenoise* that has been perfected in the small region of Champagne in north-east France. Only if it is made in this area, using this method can it be called Champagne. However, there are other excellent examples of sparkling wine produced throughout France and the world using this method but going by the name of *méthode traditionnelle* (there are other methods of producing sparkling wines too). In France, look for Crémant from the different regions; in Spain, Cava is a great value option and there are very good examples of fizz from the New World: New Zealand, Australia, Chile and South Africa etc. But, the term 'new world' is a bit misleading. There is nothing 'new' about the production of wine in these countries but some of the modern techniques they have perfected have improved wines all around the world.

Ancre Hill is a vineyard in Monmouth that I originally had in a chapter entitled 'Wines from unexpected regions'. Now even though it is not that long since the publication of the Welsh version of this book, I don't think this is an appropriate title any more, which just goes to show the rapid pace of growth of the wine industry in Wales, which is now home to more than 15 commercial vineyards. Ok, it hasn't overtaken sheep yet, but watch this space and back to Richard Morris's sparkler, which recently beat a selection of Champagnes and sparkling wines from all over the world in a competition run by a wine magazine in Italy. I rest my case.

One of my favourites is Prosecco. Produced in Italy, the second fermentation takes place in a tank and is then stopped to allow a little natural sugar to remain and produce a light, fresh and ever so slightly sweet bubbly.

An exciting development in this field is a sparkling wine from Wales that has started to win great accolades.

20   4–6

Smoked salmon and lime pinwheels

- 2 slices of bread cut lengthways
- 150g smoked salmon
- 100g soft cheese (e.g. Philadelphia)
- Juice and zest of ¼ of a lime
- Salt and pepper
- Watercress to garnish

Cling film

Simple but tasty food, this involves no cooking and are easy to serve. They also store well in the fridge if you wrap them whole in cling film. It is therefore a good idea to prepare the day before and cut just before serving. Ask your baker to slice the loaf lengthways for this recipe. You can easily adapt this dish by using pâté, or garlic and chive cheese for vegetarians.

1 Warm the cheese a little for ease of preparation.
2 Mix the cheese with the juice, zest and salt and pepper.
3 Spread the mixture onto the slices of bread like a thick layer of butter.
4 Arrange the smoked salmon on the bread, covering the cheese.
5 Cut the crust off the bread.
6 Roll the long edge of the bread quite tightly to make a cylinder shape like a Swiss roll. Wrap it tightly in cling film and place in the fridge to chill and harden.
7 When ready to serve, remove the cling film and cut into slices about 1cm thick to make the pinwheels.
8 Decorate with watercress to serve.

Wine Recommendation
Choose something to cut across the oiliness of the salmon and the fat in the cheese. It needs enough flavour to stand up to the smoked taste too, so you need acid in the wine and a good balance of strong flavoured fruit. Champagne, Prosecco or Chablis would do the trick. It's also worth trying a Riesling with its lime flavours as a match for smoked salmon.

20   14-16

Chorizo lollipops

- 4 new potatoes, boiled and sliced
- 1 chorizo sausage, sliced
- 3 peppers (1 green, 1 red, 1 yellow) cut with a small pastry cutter into discs.
- Olive oil

Cocktail sticks

New potatoes and spicy chorizo go so well together. This is so easy – just a fry and construct job, really.

1 Heat some of the olive oil in a heavy frying pan and fry the chorizo.
2 Place the chorizo to one side and fry the potatoes until brown and place to one side.
3 Fry the peppers until they begin to brown.
4 Use the cocktail sticks to construct the lollipops, using the peppers each end to keep the chorizo and potato in place.
5 Serve warm.

Wine Recommendation
If you're serving the lollipops or the Lamb Burgers on the next page as tapas, the fatty nature of these dishes needs acid and elements of tannin to combat the grease. Rioja would be a good choice in my opinion.

30   12–16

Mini Welsh lamb burgers

- 250g Welsh lamb, finely minced
- 50g leeks, finely chopped
- 50g breadcrumbs
- 1 dessertspoon fresh mint, finely chopped
- 1 egg
- Salt and pepper
- 1 tsp beef stock (powder)
- Oil for frying
- 4 slices bread
- Chutney

My father and brother in law are local farmers so I couldn't possibly neglect the excellent Welsh lamb. A plateful of these makes a good centrepiece for the tapas table. This is what we ate one New Year's Eve, along with other small platters and salad, and everyone enjoyed a relaxed evening of chomping our way to midnight. These are easily adapted to make canapés by placing them on small circles of toast or on a Chinese style spoon with the chutney. Remember to make them small enough for this.

1 Thoroughly mix all the raw ingredients in a large bowl.
2 Use a dessertspoon to shape small balls and pat gently to flatten them into a burger.
3 Heat the oil in a frying pan until it is hot enough to hear the burgers sizzle when placed in it. Fry the burgers for 3 minutes each side. Don't put too many burgers in at a time. When one batch is cooked, place them on a metal tray in the oven to keep warm.
4 Toast the bread. Cut small circles with a small pastry cutter. Spread a small amount of chutney on each circle and place the burger on top. Pile them onto a plate and serve warm.

20   4–6

Welsh Rarebit with Cwrw Llŷn (Welsh Beer)

- 250g Welsh Cheddar, grated (Hafod is among the best cheddars in Britain)
- 25g butter
- 125g smoked bacon, cut into small cubes (or 30g whole capers for vegetarian option)
- 125g leeks, finely sliced
- 2 teaspoons Worcester sauce
- 1 teaspoon Pommery mustard
- 1 tablespoon plain flour
- 80ml Brenin Enlli (King of Bardsey) Welsh beer
- 4 slices bread

Many people have their own rarebit recipe, so here is mine. I'm very fond of this simple supper and it can be served as a small tapa or canapé – it tastes even better with Welsh produce.

1   Fry the bacon in the butter for about 3 minutes.
2   Add the leeks and cook until soft.
3   Add the cheese, Worcester sauce, mustard and the flour and mix steadily until the cheese has melted.
4   Add the beer and mix well until it is totally absorbed.
5   Taste the mixture and add more salt and pepper if needed.
6   Toast the bread. Spread quite a thick layer of the mixture onto the toast and grill until it begins to brown.
7   Cut into pieces for canapés or tapas – or serve as a light supper dish with salad.

This is good with membrillo, the Spanish quince jelly that cuts through the fatty cheese beautifully. Also, I like it with toasted olive oil bread. It will store in the fridge for 2–3 weeks, just slice off what you want and soften it a bit in the microwave to use.

Wine Recommendation
The cheese in this dish is full of fat and the smoked bacon has a strong flavour so choose a big wine if you are going to eat it as tapas or supper, such as a toasty oaked Chardonnay from the New World, or Cabernet Franc from the Loire Valley. But, of course, Rarebit and Rioja would be great!

30   6–8

Glamorgan sausages

- 125g Caerphilly cheese, grated
- 125g leeks, finely sliced
- 125g fresh breadcrumbs
- 50g Parmesan cheese, grated
- 2 eggs
- 1 tablespoon fresh parsley, finely chopped
- 1 dessertspoon French mustard
- Salt and pepper

Mixture for coating sausage
- 1 bowl with plain flour, salt and pepper
- 1 egg, beaten with a bit of milk to make egg wash in a second bowl
- 125g breadcrumbs in a third bowl
- Oil to fry

Fresh breadcrumbs are essential for this recipe. Every time I have the leftovers of a white loaf I leave it for a day, then chop off the crusts and blast 3cm cubes in the food processor to make breadcrumbs and freeze it ready for any recipe that requires them: stuffing, burgers etc.

1 Mix the raw ingredients in a bowl until they are bound together. This can be a bit difficult to handle but you can add more egg if needed.
2 Take a dessertspoonful of the mixture and shape into a sausage shape. Roll it in the flour then in the egg mixture, then finally in the breadcrumbs.
3 Heat the oil in a frying pan until quite hot. The sausage should make a frying sound straight away when placed in it.
4 Keep turning the sausages until they are nicely browned all over.

Serve with a dip of some kind: mayonnaise, chutney or a tomato sauce. We took a lunchbox full of these on a staff picnic once and they were very popular!

30   12

Wild garlic choux buns

- 250ml water
- 100g butter
- 125g plain flour
- 4 eggs, beaten
- 125g soft goat's cheese
- Handful of wild garlic leaves, finely chopped
- ½ teaspoon lemon zest
- 1 teaspoon lemon juice
- Salt and pepper

Greased baking tray
Piping bag with a large-hole nozzle

Gas mark 6/200°

One sign of spring for me is the appearance of the beautiful and pungent green leaves of wild garlic growing in abundance in the Dolgellau area. A handful of these can transform an omelette or add a new dimension to salad or soup.

1   To make the dough, place the water and butter in a saucepan and bring to a rapid boil.
2   Remove from the heat. Add the sieved flour and mix well.
3   On a low heat, continue to mix until it doesn't stick to the sides and is a glossy/fatty mass.
4   Leave the mixture to cool a little.
5   Add a little of the beaten egg and mix well. Gradually repeat this until all of the egg mixture has been used.
6   Grease a baking tray and pipe marble-sized balls onto your greased baking tray. Leave about an inch between each one.
7   Bake for 20–25 minutes, until brown, thoroughly dry and firm to touch. Leave to cool.
8   Take a thin-bladed knife and pierce the flat bottom, turning it to make a small hole. Turn the oven right down and pop them back in to dry more and then remove and leave to cool completely.
9   To make the filling, mix the remaining ingredients in a bowl with salt and pepper to taste. Pipe in the cream mixture through the hole in the bottom.

It is possible to cook the choux buns days in advance and keep them in the fridge in a plastic bag, ready to pipe in the filling on the day. You can also freeze them. Other filling options are: cream cheese flavoured with garlic or chives; smoked salmon with cream cheese, or any smooth paté. You can also fill the buns with whipped cream and pour chocolate sauce over them for a dessert.

45   12–16

Fina's Tortilla

- 400g potatoes, peeled and thinly sliced
- 200g onions, thinly sliced
- 200g diced vegetables of your choice such as carrots, peppers, beans
- 4 whole cloves garlic, peeled
- 6 eggs
- ½ teaspoon mixed herbs
- Paprika (a pinch)
- Salt and pepper
- Olive oil (enough to cover the potatoes to cook)

Fairly deep, non-stick frying pan (it should comfortably hold all of the ingredients)

Many Spaniards have lived in Dolgellau over the years and have often become good friends. We try and keep in touch by visiting when we go out there. Fina was from Zaragoza and this is her version of this classic Spanish dish.

1 Sprinkle salt over the potatoes and leave for about 10 minutes. Wash off the salt and dry the potatoes with kitchen paper.
2 Heat enough olive oil in the frying pan to cover the potatoes and vegetables then add the potatoes, vegetables and garlic to the hot oil.
3 Cook slowly until the ingredients are soft but not brown.
4 Carefully, with a slotted spoon, remove the ingredients from the frying pan and place on one side. Pour the oil into a container. Remove the garlic cloves if you don't like the idea of eating a whole one, though they are quite mild after cooking. (You can save the oil to use again.)
5 Clean the frying pan and place a dessertspoon of oil in it to heat. Meanwhile, beat the eggs well in a large bowl with the herbs, paprika, salt and pepper.
6   Add the potatoes and vegetables and then pour the egg mixture into the frying pan.
7 Cook on a low heat for 5–10 minutes until it has nearly set in the middle. Use a spatula to ensure the sides and bottom are not stuck to the pan and place under a grill to finish off the cooking – it should feel firm to the touch in the middle. I usually turn it out onto a plate and then return to the pan upside down to complete the cooking but you don't have to do this.

This can be served on a slice of French bread as a tapa or canapé. It is also delicious cold for a picnic or for lunch with a salad and mayonnaise.

Wine Recommendation

A white wine from Rueda in north-west Spain is a good partner for tortilla and this could go well with the Choux Buns or the Glamorgan Sausages too because these are not big, powerful flavours but you need to complement the creamy tastes without hiding them. Go for a Sauvignon Blanc or, even better, a Verdejo – a traditional grape from that region. It is dry, fresh and lively and not too heavy.

France

LOIRE

Domaine Huet

One of our early wine trips was to the Loire in the Vouvray region to visit the renowned producer Domaine Huet. Because of the nature of our work as a couple (chef and teacher), our holidays had to be taken during half term in October and it was raining gently as we drove along the small country roads above the town trying to find the vineyard. We stopped for a while to watch the machines harvesting grapes, something we hadn't seen before at that time: a strange tractor with long legs, knocking the grapes off the vine before dropping them in a trailer.

When we finally arrived at the handsome house constructed with the same tufa stone used for the large *châteaux* of the area, it seemed deserted. However, the man himself, Gaston Huet appeared to greet us from the kitchen. It was a quiet day for them and he slowly warmed to the task of explaining the complexities of producing a white wine from the Chenin Blanc grape. Sitting in his kitchen, he took us on a wine-tasting journey of the different wines they produced from the same grape in the same place: sparkling, dry, medium and sweet. He raised his eyebrows when we mentioned the harvesting we had observed earlier in a nearby vineyard: 'What are they trying to make? Soup?'

The essential part of producing these different wines is the ability to choose clusters of grapes by hand. In order to make the sweeter wines, the winemaker needs to go through the vines and select by hand, once, twice and even three times to choose the bunches that have the correct degree of ripeness. No machines for Huet, and definitely not grapes that had been spoilt by rain!

He led us out to his very special vineyard, Le Haut Lieu, through an old metal gate between two huge trees in the

light rain, explaining how he had been busy in recent years
converting to biodynamic methods. As a result, he
maintained, the land was in much better condition,
healthier with wild flowers growing again between the
vines. He reminisced about old vintages dating back to
1887 that he had tried, again, from the same grapes, from
the same place. A man and that one patch of land
connecting us with the 19th century: its history, geography
and culture threading through the generations. As we
returned to the kitchen, he noted the cyclamen flowers
growing under the trees were dying back. The poignancy of
this simple statement struck deep with me: a man in his
eighties approaching the end of his time as the keeper of
his land.

Gathering dust in our cellar, there are two bottles of
Moelleux 1996 that I bought from him then. It is a very
special sweet wine. I'm not in a hurry to drink it, but when
I do, I shall think of Gaston and the wild flowers on the
flat land above the town of Vouvray.

BURGUNDY/BOURGOGNE

Mâcon

Connections and coincidences take you to unexpected places occasionally. During a trip to try and learn more about the special and rather complicated wines of Bourgogne (it sounds simple: all of the whites are Chardonnay and the reds Pinot Noir, but no, it is all dependent on the *terroir*) we visited an old friend, Alan Mantle, who is originally from the Dolgellau area but now lives and works as a sculptor in Mâcon. Having been to the famous vineyards in the north it was an eye opener to discover the quality of the Mâcon region at far more affordable prices. We only had to travel about five miles over the hills from Alan's studio to a wine cooperative in Azé, to discover an excellent wine that we still import today.

We also visited the Bourgogne area to stay in Beaune in 2012 with our son Tom and his wife Hayley. Imagine our excitement on seeing a shire horse being used to draw the plough between the vines in one particular vineyard. Theories of the advantages of this old-fashioned method were a hot topic of conversation between us for some time that day. What a disappointment the next day when visiting the Boisset winery and Gregory Patriat said: 'Pah! A show put on for journalists!' Ah well, I like the romantic idea and it makes a good photograph. Some do maintain that the horse's hoof is lighter on the soil, reducing the compacting effect of a machine, and there's no denying that it's 'green'!

Bourgogne is one of my favourite areas, with the pretty little villages that are home to some of the best (and most expensive) wines in the world. If you are ever there and feeling flush try and have lunch in Lameloise in Chagny. You will not regret it. You can then stroll through some of the most famous vineyards in the world by following the

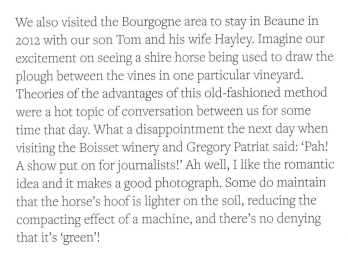

neat little signage system for walks of red, green and yellow symbols. It makes for a most relaxing, pleasurable and educational day.

Further north – an important factor in wine-making terms – a little cooler, but still in the Bourgogne region, you have the renowned Chablis vineyards. This is a small area with singular slopes that are divided into Premier Cru and Grand Cru. The white limestone soil is perfect for the Chardonnay grape and is used to make Chablis.

You can't beat local knowledge.

RHÔNE

Clairette de Die

You can't beat local knowledge. Once, when staying in a gîte (stunning design by a Swiss architect that my father adored) we ate in the only restaurant open in the village. Here, I discovered Clairette de Die for the first time and loved this soft, sweet, bubbly wine. The owner gave me the address and directions and the next morning we high-tailed it over the mountains to the vineyard where a young couple produce this singular and delicious sparkler. Frédéric and Anouck Raspail use a different technique here to the *méthode traditionnelle* seen in Champagne and other regions. The first fermentation is stopped early to prevent the yeast consuming too much sugar. Then it is bottled, capped and left for a second fermentation to produce bubbles, producing a fresh, perfumed wine with a bit of sweetness.

A word about stock and pastry

I sincerely hope that everyone will be comfortable following the recipes in this book. For this reason, I have tried to make the recipes accessible to all and keep things simple. Therefore, I have absolutely no problem with shop-bought stock. I cannot emphasise the importance of stock, be it homemade or bought in, to contribute to the flavour of cooking. It is essential.

In the recipes, I refer to powdered stock and this is available in most supermarkets or wholefood shops. It offers more flexibility than cubes or jellies and you can add as little as you like to boost flavour. If you need liquid stock then follow the maker's instructions for the required quantity.

The same goes for pastry. If buying it saves time and makes life easier for you then do so for goodness sake! Life really is too short!

Finally, salt, pepper and seasoning in general. I cannot place enough emphasis on the importance of tasting what you are cooking. Taste regularly as you cook and adapt the seasoning to suit your palate. The trick is to add a little at a time and note any changed quantities. A good well-used cookbook is covered in scribbles!

I know my wife adds a little vegetable stock powder to her omelette mixture.

30   6-8

Chinese chicken soup

- 1 tablespoon sesame oil
- 400g chicken breast, sliced into thin strips
  Slice the following vegetables into thin strips:
- 1 red pepper
- 1 yellow pepper
- 1 carrot
- 1 leek
- 2 sticks celery
- 1 onion
- 1 courgette
- 200g mushrooms
- 2 cloves garlic
- 2cm square of fresh ginger, very finely chopped
- 1 dessertspoon tomato purée
- 1lt chicken stock
- 100ml sweet sherry
- 75ml dark soy sauce
- 1 dessertspoon soft brown sugar
- 1 teaspoon mixed herbs
- 1 teaspoon 5-spice powder
- Salt and pepper
- Fresh coriander and basil to garnish

1. Heat the oil until very hot in a saucepan and quickly fry the meat.
2. Add the vegetables and ginger to the meat and fry for about 8 minutes.
3. Add the purée, sherry, stock, soy sauce, sugar, herbs and 5-spice.
4. Simmer for 5 minutes.
5. Chop the coriander and basil and sprinkle on the soup to garnish before serving.

Wine Recommendation
I served a small glass of chilled Oloroso sherry with this soup for one of our tasting menus when I had the restaurant and everyone was pleasantly surprised. The spice and saltiness of Chinese food means sherry is a good match.

30   8–10

Pistou

- 1 tablespoon olive oil
  Finely chop the following
  6 ingredients:
- 1 onion
- 2 sticks celery
- 2 leeks
- 1 red pepper
- 1 carrot
- 1 courgette
- 2lt strong vegetable
  stock
- 200g French beans
- 2 tomatoes, finely
  chopped
- 2 potatoes, finely diced
- 200g haricot beans
  (cooked)
- Salt and pepper

Paste
- 2 cloves garlic
- 1 large bunch basil
- 30g Parmesan cheese,
  grated
- 150ml olive oil

This is a lot of soup but it does keep well in the fridge. Healthy and tasty!

1 Sweat the 6 finely-chopped vegetables on a low heat for about 10 minutes.
2 Add the stock, the remainder of the vegetables and simmer for 5–10 minutes. Turn off the heat.
3 Taste and add salt and pepper but remember that the paste adds flavour too.
4 To make the paste, place the garlic, basil and Parmesan in the food processor and blend on a fairly fast speed whilst slowly adding the olive oil. Store in a container.
5 To serve, add a teaspoonful per person of the paste to the hot soup. Mix in and serve with fresh crusty bread.

30　6–8

Caldo Verde

- 1 tablespoon olive oil
- 300g quality smoked back bacon, cut into thin strips
- 1 onion, thinly sliced
- 2 cloves garlic, crushed
- 1.5lt good quality chicken or vegetable stock
- 300g potatoes, diced
- 1 small Savoy or summer cabbage, thinly sliced
- Finely chopped parsley for garnish

A traditional soup from north-west Spain and Portugal with the kind of simple ingredients that are widely available in Wales. Maybe the idea of a cabbage and bacon soup isn't instantly appealing but customers always seem to enjoy it.

1　Heat the oil in the pan and fry the bacon at a fairly high temperature.
2　Turn down the heat to medium and add the garlic and onion to sweat for 5 minutes until soft.
3　Add the stock and potatoes and simmer for 10 minutes.
4　Add the cabbage and simmer for a further 10 minutes until the cabbage is cooked.
5　Add salt and pepper carefully because of the salty nature of the bacon.

Serve with chopped fresh parsley and a drizzle of quality olive oil.

Wine Recommendation
With bread, the Pistou or the Caldo Verde can be a good main course. Try a light and fruity red wine from Italy such as Bardolino or Valpolicella.

25   6-8

Pen Llŷn crab chowder

- 50g butter
- 2 carrots
- 1 onion
- 1 leek
- 2 sticks celery
- 1 teaspoon tomato purée
- 1 dessertspoon plain flour
- 2 x 200g tin sweetcorn
- ½lt double cream
- 1lt fish or vegetable stock
- 1 teaspoon mixed herbs
- Salt and pepper
- 500g crab meat
- Fresh parsley, finely chopped

This is a luxurious treat for lunch or serve a small bowl as a starter before a light main course.

1 Melt the butter and sweat the finely chopped vegetables over a gentle heat for about 10 minutes.
2 Add the purée and the flour and mix them thoroughly with a wooden spoon. The mixture will thicken as you mix.
3 Slowly add the stock a little at a time, mixing each lot in completely and allowing it to thicken before adding the next to avoid lumps.
4 Add one tin of sweetcorn and simmer for 5 minutes.
5 Remove the saucepan from the heat. Place half of the mixture in the food processor and blend until smooth. Return to the saucepan. You now have the consistency of chowder.
6 Add the second tin of sweetcorn, salt and pepper, herbs and the cream. Bring it back to simmer for 5 minutes.
7 Add the crabmeat and once again, bring back to simmering point and take off the heat.

Serve with a generous sprinkling of parsley and bread.

Wine Recommendation
With this rich dish you need a wine to withstand the strong flavours. Riesling, possibly from Alsace but please don't forget the German Rieslings, which are out of fashion but make wonderful drinking: full of flavour and enough acid to cut across the cream.

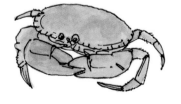

40   8–10

Pork and cranberry pâté

- 250g minced pork
- 250g belly pork
- 250g gammon
- 250g pig's liver
- 1 medium onion, finely chopped
- 1 clove garlic, crushed
- 1 teaspoon mixed herbs
- 1 egg
- 1 teaspoon salt and pepper
- 50g dried cranberries
- 50g pistachio nuts

Half kilo bread tin or terrine
Roasting tin
Greaseproof paper/ foil

Gas mark 4/190°C

1 Place the minced pork in a large bowl.
2 With a sharp knife, dice the gammon and the belly pork.
3 Then, one at a time, blend the gammon and the belly pork in a food processor. The consistency of your pâté will depend on the length of time you blend, whether you want a smooth or coarse pâté.
4 Dice the liver finely and process until smooth. Add the onion and garlic and blend again.
5 Add the liver mixture to the bowl and mix with the remainder of the ingredients.
6 Line the baking tin with greaseproof paper and put the mixture in it. Cover the tin with foil.
7 Place the terrine in the roasting tin and pour hot water up to about halfway of the roasting tin. Cover the roasting pan and tin with foil.
8 Carefully place in the oven and cook for 1½ hours.
9 Remove from the oven and leave in cold water to cool. If it has risen, place a board and a weight on it to press it down and firm it up.
10 Turn out of the baking tin after it has cooled and place in the fridge. This will keep in the fridge for several days.

Eat this with toast and some kind of pickle. Cranberry sauce or Cumberland sauce with orange is also a good match, served with a bit of salad.

40   12

Chicken and ham terrine

- 500g chicken breast
- 2 egg whites
- 500g ham, cooked and diced to 1cm cubes
- 100g gherkins, diced into 1cm pieces
- 300ml double cream
- ½ teaspoon salt
- ¼ teaspoon paprika
- ¼ teaspoon ground cumin
- Pepper

Terrine tin

Gas mark 4/180°

Terrine is the French word for the cooking pot and I still use the one my friend Peter Jackson made for me in his pottery classes about 20 years ago!

1 Blend the chicken meat in a food processor.
2 Add the egg white and seasoning and blend again.
3 Pour the mixture into a large bowl and fold in the cream.
4 Fold in the gherkins and ham.
5 Line the tin with cling film and pour in the mixture, pressing down firmly to avoid any air bubbles.
6 Cover with cling film and then with foil.
7 Place the terrine in a roasting tin and then fill the roasting tin with hot water up to about halfway of the terrine. Cover the whole thing with foil.
8 Place on the hob and bring the water to the boil before placing in the oven.
9 Cook for about an hour until cooked through and is firm to touch.
10 Leave to cool before removing from the tin. Wrap in cling film and store in the fridge ready for use.

Serve with a sweet sauce like Cumberland or with mayonnaise mixed with a grainy mustard.

40   8

Faggot

- 500g pig's liver
- 200g belly pork, finely chopped
- 60g suet
- 60g breadcrumbs
- 1 onion, finely chopped
- Pinch of nutmeg
- 1 teaspoon sage
- 1 teaspoon salt
- ¼ teaspoon pepper

Foil
Greaseproof paper
Bread tin

Gas mark 6/200°C

Faggot has a bit of a poor image but this recipe is like a good French terrine and I learnt it from Dora Jones who lived opposite me in Arthog when I was young and living alone. Many was the time I would arrive home from work to find a plate of delicious food for me on the doorstep, sometimes a slice of faggot with a few of her husband Owen's superb little home grown tomatoes!

1. Cut out the tubes from the liver and throw them away, leaving the tender pieces.
2. Place in the food processor and blend until smooth.
3. Add the pork and onion to the liver in the processor and blend again for a short time.
4. Place the remainder of the ingredients in a large bowl and add the meat. Mix well.
5. Place the mixture in a baking tin that has been lined with greaseproof paper and cover with foil.
6. Bake for 45 minutes. Remove the paper and bake for a further 15 minutes to brown the top.

This is delicious served cold with apple sauce with some spice in it.

Wine Recommendation
These pâtés and terrines make lovely light lunches in the summer time with a salad and light fruity reds with a bit of acidity would match well. Beaujolais comes to mind, or what about the erstwhile Parisian bistro favourite Saumur-Champigny.

30   6

Mushroom pâté

- 250g mushrooms, finely chopped
- 50g butter
- 50g soft white breadcrumbs
- 2 teaspoons onion, very finely chopped
- 80g soft butter
- 125g mild soft cheese
- ½ teaspoon lemon zest
- 1 teaspoon lemon juice
- 1 teaspoon mushroom powder (Snowdonia Mushrooms)
- ¼ teaspoon ground nutmeg
- Salt and pepper

Six ramekins or small bowls

1 In a saucepan, melt the butter and gently cook the mushrooms on a medium heat until they are soft. Mix with a wooden spoon – there is no need to fry or brown them. Leave the mixture to cool a little.

2 Place in the food processor and carefully blend, ensuring that you leave small pieces of mushroom visible in the mixture.

3 Place the remainder of the ingredients in the food processor and blend again quickly just to mix everything.

4 Using a spoon, carefully place the mixture in small ramekins. It is easier to use a piping bag. You can also pipe small portions onto toast to make canapés.

5 Place in the fridge to chill and eat with toast and salad.

Wine Recommendation
The earthy flavour of mushrooms can be difficult to pair with wine. Grapes such as Nebbiolo or Pinot Noir can work.

30   6

Salmon and prawn pasties

- Packet of puff pastry
- 250g salmon and prawns, chopped into small pieces
- 100g potatoes, finely diced
- 100g half and half leek and onion, finely chopped
- 50g melted butter
- 1 teaspoon lemon zest and juice
- ½ teaspoon dried tarragon
- 1 egg, beaten
- Salt and pepper

Greased baking tray

Gas mark 6/200°C

1 Roll the pastry and cut into 15 cm discs – a total of six.
2 Mix all the ingredients together except for the egg.
3 To seal the pastry brush the discs with the beaten egg.
4 It is possible to buy a pasty maker but if you don't have one, put a dessertspoon of the mixture on the middle of the disc and fold to make a pasty shape.
5. Using a fork press down the sides to seal the edges.
6 Brush the pasty again with the beaten egg to give it colour and make a small hole in the top with a knife to release any steam when it is cooking.
7 Place the pasties on the baking tray and cook for 15–20 minutes until they are brown.

Serve with tartare sauce or lime mayonnaise and a mixed salad.

30   6

Chicken and apple turnover

- 300g chicken meat, diced
- 200g sausage meat
- 75g onion, finely chopped
- 75g leeks, finely chopped
- 75g celery, finely chopped
- Oil for cooking
- 1 eating apple, peeled and finely chopped
- ½ teaspoon of thyme (dried or fresh)
- 1 teaspoon chicken stock powder
- Salt and pepper
- 1 egg yolk
- Packet puff pastry, rolled ready to 35cm x 25cm
- Black poppy seeds for sprinkling on top of the turnover before cooking
- Egg wash

Oblong baking tray
45cm x 25cm

Gas mark 6/200°C

1   Place a little oil in a frying pan and cook the onions, celery and leek for 5–10 minutes or until they are soft. Allow to cool for a while.

2   Place all the vegetables with the remainder of the ingredients in a bowl (except for the black poppy seeds and the egg wash) and mix well.

3   Put the puff pastry on the greased baking tray and line the mixture down the middle, ready to make a large sausage shape.

4   Fold one side over the mixture and brush with a little egg wash, then fold the other side over and gently press down to seal.

5   Gently rotate the turnover so that the sealed line is now underneath.

6   Brush the turnover with the egg wash and sprinkle a generous layer of the poppy seeds over it.

7   Bake for 25–30 minutes.

This is perfect for picnics as well as a first course, with a salad or some kind of pickle.

50   8

Sundried tomato quiche

Savoury pastry

- 225g plain flour
- 115g cold butter
- ½ teaspoon mixed herbs
- Salt and pepper
- 1 egg
- 1 dessertspoon cold water

25cm loose base flan tin
Greaseproof paper

Filling

- 300g mixed vegetables, finely chopped
- 5 eggs
- 330ml double cream
- 125g grated cheddar
- 125g semi-dried tomatoes
- Handful fresh basil, roughly chopped
- Salt and pepper

Gas mark 4/180°C

Savoury pastry

1 Combine the flour and butter in a food processor (or rub the butter into the flour by hand).
2 Add the seasoning and the mixed herbs.
3 Add the egg and water and process, or mix by hand to form a ball.
4 Wrap in cling film and put in the fridge for half an hour.
5 Roll out the pastry thinly on a floured surface.
6 Line the greased tin with the pastry and pierce the bottom with a fork before baking it blind – you must bake the pastry before adding the filling. Cover the pastry with greaseproof paper and fill it with ceramic peas or you may use dried peas. This will prevent the pastry from rising.
7 Cook for 30–45 minutes.

Filling

1 Heat a little oil in a frying pan and sweat the vegetables until they are soft.
2 In a bowl large enough to hold all of the ingredients, mix the eggs and cream together.
3 Add all the ingredients to the cream mixture putting aside a little cheese for the topping.
4 Fill the pastry case with the mixture and sprinkle the cheese on top.
5 Place in the oven and cook for about 30 minutes until the middle has set.

30   6

Tomato, goat's cheese and basil tart

- 3 tablespoons olive oil
- 500g onions, thinly sliced
- 2 cloves garlic
- Tin of chopped tomatoes
- 1 dessertspoon tomato purée
- 1 dessertspoon sugar
- 1 teaspoon mixed herbs
- 1 teaspoon vegetable stock powder
- Salt and pepper
- 250g goat's cheese (quite a hard cheese such as Pant Mawr) diced into small cubes.
- 250g Cheddar cheese, grated
- Handful of basil leaves, chopped
- Olive oil
- Salt and pepper
- Packet of puff pastry

Greased baking tray
45cm x 25cm

Gas mark 6/200°C

This tomato mixture keeps well in the fridge and you can use it to make pizzas or pissaladière – a traditional southern French tart with anchovies on top.

1 Heat the oil in a saucepan. Slowly soften the onions and garlic for 15–20 minutes occasionally stirring to avoid burning.
2 Add the purée, tomatoes, sugar, mixed herbs, the stock and salt and pepper.
3 Cook gently for about 15 minutes, until the mixture has thickened.
4 Roll the pastry thinly to create a 20cm x 35cm piece.
5 Spread the mixture fairly thinly onto the pastry leaving a gap of about 1cm around the edges.
6 Dot the goat's cheese over the tomato mixture, then sprinkle on the basil and lastly the Cheddar cheese.
7 Drizzle a little olive oil over the tart and a little salt and pepper.
8 Bake in a hot oven for about 20 minutes or until the pastry is cooked in the middle.

Eat this with a rocket salad and the best tomatoes.

Wine Recommendation
You have to be careful when pairing tomatoes with wine because of their acidic nature, thus you need to have a wine to match that. Italian wines also tend to have a high acidity. Choose something like a Valpolicella or a Barbera.

15   4

Crab and avocado salad

- 350g crabmeat, brown and white
- 2 avocados, diced
- 2 tablespoons mayonnaise
- ½ lime, zest and juice
- 125g small tomatoes, cucumber and red pepper, finely chopped
- Salt and pepper
- Handful of fresh coriander, roughly chopped

1 Quite simply, mix all the ingredients except the coriander.
2 Place on a plate and sprinkle the coriander over the salad.

This is delicious with crusty bread and a green salad.

Wine Recommendation
For my father in law John's birthday, we ate this with a delicious German Riesling: a light wine, full of fruit and low in alcohol that is a little sweet but with a good balance of acidity. The match was perfect.

10

4

Sugarsnap peas, orange and cucumber salad

- 150g sugarsnap peas
- 150g cucumber, cut into long strips
- 1 large orange, cut into segments
- ¼ iceberg lettuce

Dressing
- Salad oil
- 1 orange, zest and juice
- 1 piece stem ginger, cut into very thin strips
- White wine vinegar
- Sugar
- 1 teaspoon French mustard
- Salt and pepper

Credit for adding the sugarsnap peas to this salad has to be given to Emma, our long-standing, long-suffering front of house and now blossoming wine expert, who has been with us for over 20 years. Use a very sharp knife to cut and segment the orange.

1 Boil a pan of water and throw in the sugarsnap peas for 1 to 2 minutes only. Cool them quickly by putting in cold water. If they are large, cut them in half.
2 Mix all the ingredients to make the dressing.
3 Combine all the salad ingredients, add salt and pepper before pouring the dressing over just before serving. Make sure every portion has small pieces of ginger.

10   4

Beetroot, goat's cheese and pumpkin seed salad

- 250g boiled beetroot, cut into cubes
- 150g goat's cheese
- 50g red onion, thinly sliced
- 50g pumpkin seeds, toasted
- Pumpkin seed oil
- Balsamic vinegar
- Mixed salad leaves
- Sea salt and pepper

I am famous in our family for ranting at the TV and newspaper when I believe they offer recipes that are not recipes. I suppose the following is that kind of recipe!

1   Mix the beetroot, goat's cheese, onion and seeds together and add the sea salt and pepper.
2   Simply drizzle the oil and vinegar evenly over the salad.

Wine Recommendation
Frequently, you will hear the words 'crisp and dry' when talking about wine and that is exactly what these two leafy salads are crying out for. Any Sauvignon would be good, such as the French classic Sancerre from the Loire Valley or one from New Zealand..

Spain

RIOJA

The pleasure of visiting Javier is a good enough reason for buying wine in Baja Rioja – an area that traditionally grows more of the Garnacha (Grenache) grape. These grapes are usually seen as inferior for producing wine of the best quality in Rioja. However, Javier has mostly planted his vineyard with the Tempranillo grape. The best quality often comes from the oldest vines, despite the fact that they produce fewer and fewer grapes as they age. Javier's father used to sell his grapes to a local cooperative but by now, the development of the business has allowed him to buy his own equipment to establish his own *bodega*. Even though his unit is neat and tidy and meticulously clean, it is not comparable with the new mansions in the Alta region like the one in the picture on page 95. So it is interesting to note that it is these very same famous companies that occasionally come knocking on Javier's door to buy his wine to add to their own!

Some of the vines in his vineyards are over 50 years old.

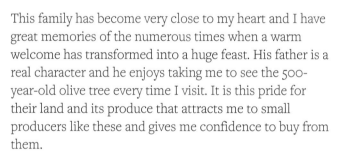

This family has become very close to my heart and I have great memories of the numerous times when a warm welcome has transformed into a huge feast. His father is a real character and he enjoys taking me to see the 500-year-old olive tree every time I visit. It is this pride for their land and its produce that attracts me to small producers like these and gives me confidence to buy from them.

On one occasion, I had an appointment to see him in March (not the best time to visit but that's the way it used to be when running a restaurant) and the overnight snow was such that I was forced to buy snow chains for the car so that I could get out of Soria where I had stayed the previous night. The minute I arrived I could feel excitement in the air and Javier mischievously informed me it was a *fiesta* because of the snow and there would be no work in the *bodega* that day. I arrived at his house in time to join about twenty of his family and their children,

to enjoy a big family meal of traditional foods set out on a huge table in the garage. Good humour and the spirit of generosity were, and always are, in the air as the wine and spirits flowed.

Another time, I had to wait for some important customers from Catalunya to leave before Javier set some vine twigs in the fireplace in the corner of the tasting room to light a fire. He cooked tiny lamb chops on this fire and we both sat to taste some of his wines whilst munching our way through a pile of these chops with chorizo, Serrano ham, salad and bread. Such a pleasurable way to do business!

A Tapas Tour of Toro

Another memorable trip to Spain was to meet Nicola, an English woman who has settled in the Toro region. It is a little further down river from one of the most expensive and famous regions of Spain these days that is Ribera del Duero. Duero is the Spanish name for the same river Douro in Portugal that finishes its journey in the Atlantic at Oporto. Toro is growing in popularity as a region that produces high quality red wines at a reasonable price. At that time, Nicola was working for Bajoz, at the brand new and large *bodega* just outside the town.

After tasting the wines, she led me and the brave German girl who was studying Spanish in Salamanca, on a tour of the tapas bars in the town. One bar was in a building that had cellars dug deep into the rock below, going at least two floors underground. Health and safety did cross my mind as I did a quick risk assessment for fire evacuation in an emergency. Their uses by now have been diversified and this particular bar held regular discos!

The choice of wines available to buy by the glass there was amazing and this is partly what I want to try and replicate in Dolgellau. People would come in and ask for their favourite wine from a local producer. In one bar, Nicola noticed an uncleared table with an empty decanter in the middle. She took a deep sniff of the decanter and guessed the wine and the producer. The waiter confirmed that she was spot on! This kind of natural expertise is so impressive.

On this particularly pleasurable night out, Nicola, who is a vegetarian, was choosing our tapas but not revealing the ingredients until after we had eaten them. She was eager for me to sample regional specialities. I guessed most correctly, but one I will not be trying again is *Morro de ternaera* – cow's lips!

The town is full of cellars like these where wine was produced for centuries.

30   6

Welsh lamb casserole and Snowdonia mushrooms

- 1kg Welsh lamb, diced
- 500g onion, chopped
- 250g celery, chopped
- 250g carrots chopped
- 500g shiitake mushrooms
- 1 tablespoon plain flour
- Salt and pepper
- 1 teaspoon dried thyme
- 500ml beef stock or lamb stock
- Oil for frying

Gas mark 5/190°C

I make no apologies for including three Welsh lamb recipes in this book. This is what people really used to enjoy in the restaurant – tourists and locals alike loved the lamb that is bred naturally on the hills of Wales.

1   Warm the oil in a frying pan and brown the meat, a few pieces at a time, and place them in a casserole dish.
2   After frying all the meat, heat another tablespoon of oil in the frying pan and gently fry all the vegetables until soft.
3   Add the flour, salt and pepper and thyme and mix well.
4   Add the stock a little at a time and mix well to thicken the mixture.
5   Add the mixture to the lamb in the casserole dish. If the mixture is a little too thick, add more stock.
6   Cook in the oven for about an hour and a half until the meat is tender.

It is possible to use different kinds of mushrooms. From June onwards, I sometimes gather a limited range of wild mushrooms like chanterelle or boletus (my friend Georges generously showed me where to find chanterelle) but there is a wide variety available in shops and supermarkets these days. I bought these from the Mushroom Garden in Nantmor.

Wine Recommendation
Red wine that is not too full-bodied would be a good match here; a fairly light wine that doesn't affect the delicate taste of the wild mushrooms in the casserole but has enough acid to cut across the fat in the lamb. Any Pinot Noir would be suitable, and it would be possible to get the same autumnal flavours with an old Burgundy.

30   6–8

Riojan lamb

- 2kg boned leg of lamb
- 1 onion, sliced
- 250ml lamb stock
- 250ml Rioja (or any good quality red wine)
- 1 teaspoon dried thyme
- 1 teaspoon beef stock powder
- 1 dessertspoon cornflour
- Salt and pepper

Gas mark 5/190°C

1 Ask your butcher to bone and roll a leg of lamb and trim it well. Keep the bone and the trimmings to make the stock.

2 Make the stock in advance by boiling the meat and trimmings. Skim the fat from the top of the stock and keep to one side.

3 Place some of the fat in a roasting tin and heat it on the hob. (Take care to do this in a roasting pan that can take the heat, otherwise use a frying pan.)

4 Brown the rolled lamb in the fat and seal it well.

5 Remove the lamb from the roasting tin and put to one side.

6 Add the onion to the fat and cook until lightly browned.

7 Return the lamb to the roasting tin, add the stock, stock powder and wine.

8 Add the thyme and salt and pepper.

9 Cover with foil and place in the oven for 2½ hours. During cooking, remove at least once to turn the leg of lamb.

10 Remove from the oven and put the gravy into a saucepan. Cover the lamb and leave to rest whilst you finish the gravy.

11 Boil the gravy to reduce it, skimming the fat off the top. You may thicken the gravy with some cornflour mixed with water.

12 Slice quite thick tranches of the meat to serve with the gravy.

This is delicious served with red cabbage and roast potatoes or creamy mash.

45   6-8

Lamb, Port, plum and ginger pie

- 2.5kg leg of lamb – the bone completely removed and the meat cut into 2.5cm cubes
- 2 tablespoons oil
- 2 onions, chopped
- 2 carrots, finely diced
- 4 sticks celery, finely diced
- 1 tablespoon plain flour
- 1 tablespoon tomato purée
- 375ml Port
- 4 pieces stem ginger, finely chopped
- 1 tablespoon syrup from jar
- 450g plums, stoned and roughly chopped
- 500ml lamb or beef stock
- 1 teaspoon thyme
- Puff pastry – enough to cover the top of the casserole dish
- Salt and pepper

Gas mark 4/180°C

This recipe requires stem ginger in syrup that is available in jars. The ginger counteracts the fattiness, and the syrup matches the sweetness of the lamb. Ask your butcher to cut the bone out of the leg and then you can use it to make stock along with the other spare trimmings.

1 Heat the oil in a frying pan and brown the meat, a few pieces at a time. Place the pieces in the bottom of a casserole or pie dish.
2 Add the onions, carrots and celery to the frying pan and fry for a few minutes.
3 Add the flour to the frying pan and mix with the vegetables before adding the purée. Mix the ingredients well.
4 Add the Port and stock, a little at a time, and mix well. This will thicken the mixture.
5 Then add the salt and pepper, thyme, ginger and syrup.
6 Pour this over the lamb and place in an oven for about an hour and a half or cook on top of the stove.
7 Remove from the oven and add the plums to the casserole.
8 Cover the dish with the pastry, pinching around the edges to seal. With a knife, cut a hole in the middle of the pastry to allow steam to escape.
9 Return to the oven and cook for 30–40 minutes until the pastry is brown.

Wine Recommendation
Some of the classic food and wine combinations are often those developed over time in particular regions. Rioja and lamb is one such marriage that works so well.

There are different levels of Rioja: Joven is a young wine that hasn't been aged in oak barrels; Crianza, which is the first quality level that has been aged in oak barrels; Reserva has had more time in barrel and bottle, finally the Gran Reserva, which has had even more time in the oak barrels and bottle and cannot be released before 7 years after the harvest. It can become more complex as the various producers make special cuvées that don't necessarily follow the rules but are often wonderful wines.

30   4

- 4 steaks, 240g each
- Oil to fry

Pommery sauce
- 70ml white wine
- 125ml beef stock
- 125ml cream
- 4 teaspoons Pommery mustard
- Salt and pepper

Oven on low heat for the steak to rest

Ask for sirloin that has been hung for at least three weeks.

Steak with Pommery sauce

When I asked staff and customers which recipes they would like to see in the book, steak and sauces were repeatedly requested. A good steak always begins with hanging the meat. There is not much any chef can do to improve this.

My favourite method for cooking the steak is in a hot frying pan. This way, you will have all the flavours of the steak in the pan in the remaining juices. The flavour of the sauce is totally dependent on the reduction. This simply means boiling the liquid at a high temperature to reduce and thicken, to intensify the flavour.

You need to experiment with the cooking times for steak because there are many factors at play here that can change it: the thickness of the piece of meat is the essential factor and of course the temperature of the frying pan. I like a medium rare steak and for 240g steak about 2cm thick, I fry for about three minutes each side.

1   Heat the frying pan until the oil is hot and place the steak in it carefully. Add the steak to be cooked the most well done first.
2   Cook the steak for about three minutes on one side depending on personal preference.
3   Turn the steak over and cook on the other side for the same amount of time.
4   Place the steaks in the oven to rest and keep warm.
5   Add the wine to the pan and with a wooden spoon simmer the wine and 'clean' the pan. This is called deglazing.
6   Add the stock and cook the sauce to reduce until it has nearly all disappeared. To achieve this it must reach a high cooking point.
7   Add the cream, Pommery mustard and the salt and pepper. Reduce the mixture once again. The texture should be thick and creamy.
8   Pour over the steak and serve immediately.

20

4

Two more steak sauces

Mushroom and Madeira sauce

- 25 g butter
- 1 onion, finely diced
- 250g mushrooms, thinly sliced
- 1 dessertspoon tomato purée
- 1 dessertspoon plain flour
- 250ml Madeira
- 250ml beef stock
- ½ teaspoon thyme
- Salt and pepper

You may prepare these two sauces in advance and keep them in the fridge. Cook the steak using the same method as the previous page and clean the pan (deglaze) with red wine. Then, add a large tablespoon of sauce for each person and add to the reduced red wine. Heat and pour over steak.

I used to use plain flour in both of these sauces, however, with the frequency of medical conditions such as coeliac, I tend to use a mixture of cornflour and water to thicken the sauce.

1 Melt the butter and add the onions to brown so that they caramelise slowly but don't burn. This can take up to 15 minutes.
2 Add the mushrooms and cook until soft.
3 Mix in the tomato purée with the onions and mushrooms.
4 Add the flour and mix in well before adding the stock and Madeira, a little at a time.
5 Add the thyme and the salt and pepper.
6 Simmer for 20–30 minutes.
7 Taste the mixture to check for seasoning.
8 Leave to chill and store in the fridge until needed.

In the early days of the restaurant I told my wife for a bit of a joke that we would have to call this recipe Claret and Blue sauce. Now, writing the book she asked, 'What joke?' I realised my humour had fallen on deaf ears for 25 years. I was born and brought up in Essex and our local football team was West Ham. One of the team nicknames was, and still is, Claret and Blue, hence the name of the sauce. Oh, well! Unlike the football team, this sauce is always strong and very rich!

1 Melt the butter and fry the onions until soft but not brown.
2 Add the Claret and the stock and boil rapidly to reduce to half.
3 Add the cream and mix in the cheeses.
4 Mix the cornflour in a cup with a little bit of cold water until it is a smooth liquid. Stir in to the simmering sauce so that it thickens.
5 Allow the mixture to cool a little before placing in a food processor and blending until smooth.
6 Leave to chill and store in the refrigerator until it is needed. It will keep for a few days.

Wine Recommendation

Claret is the English name for red wines from Bordeaux. Virtually all are blended wines, predominantly Cabernet Sauvignon and Merlot. Whether steaks or roast, it's the type of wine to which I turn, whether from Bordeaux itself or others of a similar style from around the world. Here, the balance of fruit, acidity and tannins can stand up to the protein and rich sauces.

Claret and Blue sauce

- 25g butter
- 1 onion, finely chopped
- 250ml Claret (or any red wine)
- 250ml beef stock
- 125ml double cream
- 70g Perl Las cheese (rind removed and chopped into small cubes)
- 70g Roquefort cheese, cubed
- Salt and pepper (but remember that the cheese is salty)
- 1 teaspoon cornflour

40   4

Spicy meatballs

Meatballs

- 500g minced beef
- ½ onion, finely chopped
- ½ red pepper, very finely chopped
- 90g breadcrumbs
- 1 teaspoon mixed herbs
- 1 clove garlic, crushed
- 1 teaspoon beef stock powder
- 1 egg
- ½ teaspoon ground cumin
- ½ teaspoon paprika
- Salt and pepper
- Oil to fry

Sauce

- Olive oil
- 1 onion
- 1 green pepper
- 2 sticks celery
- 1 clove garlic, crushed
- 1 tin tomatoes
- 1 dessertspoon tomato purée
- 250ml beef stock
- 1 teaspoon mixed herbs
- 1 dessertspoon sugar
- 1 teaspoon paprika
- Salt and pepper

Meatballs

1 Mix the ingredients in a large bowl.
2 Using a dessertspoon, form the mixture into small balls.
3 Heat the olive oil in a large frying pan.
4 Brown the meatballs on a fairly high temperature, a few at a time.
5 Place the meatballs to one side while you make the sauce.

Sauce

1 In the same frying pan (there is no need to wash) add oil to heat if needed.
2 Thinly slice the onion, green pepper and celery before frying them with the garlic until soft.
3 Add the purée and the tomatoes and mix well into the softened vegetables before adding the stock.
4 Add the remainder of the ingredients.
5 Gently place the meatballs in the sauce, making sure that they are well covered.
6 Simmer for 20 minutes.

Serve with rice or crusty bread.

30   4–6

Boston pork and beans

- 600g pork, diced
- 150g smoked bacon, finely diced
- 2 carrots
- 1 small red pepper
- 1 onion
- 2 sticks celery
- 2 cloves garlic, crushed
- 1 dessertspoon tomato purée
- 1 tin chopped tomatoes
- 500ml chicken stock
- 1 dessertspoon treacle
- 1 teaspoon mixed herbs
- 250g butter beans, cooked
- Salt and pepper
- Oil to fry

This is one of my mother's recipes. Sadly, she did not have much time to teach me, but she instilled in me a love of cooking. My first job at home was to make the gravy for Sunday lunch and I remember standing on a chair to mix flour into the fat in the roasting tin, using water from the vegetables to add flavour. This recipe kept me going through my three years at Exeter University (I would eat it for maybe four or five nights in a row). Packed with goodness and real comfort food on a cold night.

1 Heat the oil in a frying pan and brown the meat, a little at a time, and place in a saucepan. If needed, add a little more oil to fry the bacon and add to the meat in the saucepan.
2 Fry the sliced vegetables to soften before adding the purée, the tomatoes and the rest of the ingredients, except for the butter beans.
3 Mix well and pour over the meat.
4 Cook on the stove for about an hour and a quarter until the pork is tender. Add more water if needed.
5 Add the butter beans and cook for a further 15 minutes.

Eat with fresh bread or rice.

Wine Recommendation
I was not familiar with wine when I was at university but a good mature, full-bodied red wine with plenty of dark fruit flavours will be a perfect match. I would choose a Zinfandel from California or a Malbec from Argentina.

20   4

Chicken with pine nuts and sherry

- 8 chicken thighs or similar pieces
- 1 dessertspoon oil
- 1 large onion, finely chopped
- 2 sticks celery, finely chopped
- 150ml sherry
- 300ml chicken stock
- 50g sultanas
- 1 teaspoon thyme
- Salt and pepper
- 50g pine nuts, toasted

1   Heat the oil in a large frying pan and brown the pieces of chicken. Cook the skin side first.
2   Add the onions and celery to the frying pan to soften.
3   Return the chicken pieces to the frying pan and add the sherry, stock, seasoning, sultanas and thyme.
4   Simmer with the lid on for about 20 minutes.
5   If you like a thicker sauce, add a teaspoon of cornflour mixed in the little cold water and stir into the sauce.
6   Scatter the pine nuts over the chicken just before serving.

Wine Recommendation
There would be nothing wrong with a glass of one of the lighter sherries with this dish.

30   4

Chicken with spinach and coconut

- 1 dessertspoon light oil
- 500g chicken, cut into 2cm cubes
- 1 onion, finely chopped
- 2 sticks celery, finely chopped
- 125ml white wine
- 125ml chicken stock
- 250g spinach
- 1 tin coconut milk
- 250g cream cheese
- 1 dessertspoon cornflour
- Salt and pepper

1 Heat the oil in a saucepan and soften the onion and celery.
2 Add the chicken and cook to seal it.
3 Add the wine, stock, and salt and pepper.
4 Place a lid on the saucepan and simmer for 15 minutes.
5 Add the spinach and the coconut milk.
6 Add the soft cheese.
7 If you need to thicken the mixture, add the cornflour mixed in a little cold water.

Serve with pasta or rice with crunchy green vegetables.

30   4

Chicken with leek and Pernod sauce

Sauce
- 25g butter
- ½ onion, finely chopped
- 1 stick celery, finely chopped
- 125g leeks, finely sliced
- 125ml white wine
- 125ml chicken stock
- 125ml double cream

Chicken
- 4 chicken breasts
- One dessertspoon light oil
- 25ml Pernod
- Salt and pepper

Sauce
1. Melt the butter in a saucepan and sweat the onion, celery and leek.
2. Add the wine and stock and boil to reduce by half.
3. Add the cream and seasoning and reduce again. Place this to one side while you cook the chicken.

Chicken
1. In a frying pan, fry the chicken breasts on both sides until brown. This should take about five minutes on both sides.
2. Place the lid on the frying pan and leave to cook for a further 10 minutes, taking care not to burn them. You may add a little stock and wine to the bottom of the pan to avoid this.
3. Carefully pour the Pernod over the chicken breasts and return to a simmering heat.
4. Remove the chicken breasts and keep warm in the oven.
5. Pour the sauce into the frying pan to reheat and mix with the juices.
6. To serve, pour the sauce on to the plate and place a chicken breast on it.

Wine Recommendation
For rich, creamy chicken dishes, many white wines would fit the bill. Why not experiment with a Grüner Veltliner from Austria rather than a Burgundy?

30   6

Keralan monkfish and prawn curry

- 50 g butter
- 1 red pepper, thinly sliced
- 1 yellow pepper, thinly sliced
- 1 courgette, thinly sliced
- 1 onion, thinly sliced
- 1 carrot, sliced into thin batons
- 1 stick celery, thinly sliced
- 2 cloves garlic, crushed
- 2cm ginger, finely chopped
- 1 dessertspoon of each of the following powders: coriander, cumin, turmeric, paprika
- 1 dessertspoon curry paste
- 1 dessertspoon flour
- 500ml fish stock or vegetable stock
- 1 400g tin coconut milk
- Salt and black pepper
- 160g prawns and skinned and filleted monkfish per person, cut into chunks
- Handful fresh coriander, chopped
- Oil to cook

I used to enjoy travelling with my father but one country that he would not return to was India, after his experience there during the Second World War. When I did manage to make it there I visited some of the places he'd sweated away in during the war and even found the hospital in the hills by Uti where he was sent to while suffering from jaundice. I loved their careful use of light aromatic spices in southern India. This sauce can be made in advance and it takes very little time to cook the fish.

1 Melt the butter in a saucepan and cook the vegetables until soft.
2 Add the spices, salt and plenty of black pepper, then the flour and mix in well.
3 Carefully add the stock, a little at a time, mixing carefully and allowing the mixture to thicken each time before adding the next lot.
4 Pour in the coconut milk and simmer for 10 minutes.
5 Leave to cool and store in the fridge.

To cook the fish
1 Heat oil in a frying pan and fry the pieces of monkfish for a few minutes.
2 Add enough sauce for each person and bring back to simmer for a couple of minutes. Do not overcook the fish.
3 Add the prawns and heat before adding fresh coriander just before serving.

Wine Recommendation
The wine I really enjoy with this dish is a Riesling from Austria or Alsace: it is powerful and the lime flavours complement the spices. I suggest you have some fun experimenting with floral and aromatic wines such as Pinot Gris or Gewürztraminer with light curries or Asian dishes.

30   4

Hake with pea and mint sauce

- 30g butter
- 1 small onion, finely diced
- 1 stick celery, finely diced
- 125ml white wine
- 125ml fish or vegetable stock
- 200g frozen peas
- 125ml double cream
- 1 dessertspoon fresh mint, finely chopped
- 1 teaspoon mint sauce
- Salt and pepper
- Slice of lemon
- 4 x 160g hake fillets

1. Melt the butter in a saucepan and sweat the onion and celery slowly for a few minutes until soft.
2. Add the stock, seasoning and white wine and bring to the boil.
3. Add the peas and simmer for about 10 minutes.
4. Blend the mixture in a food processor to make the sauce. If you prefer a smooth sauce, push through a sieve as well, but this is not essential.
5. Place the sauce back in the saucepan and add the cream, mint and mint sauce.
6. Bring the mixture back to the boil.
7. Heat water in a deep frying pan with a little salt and pepper and a slice of lemon.
8. Place the fish into the water and simmer slowly for a few minutes with the lid on – no more than five minutes once the liquid is simmering, depending on the thickness of the fish.
9. Put the fish on a plate to serve and pour the sauce over it.

30   4

Paprika salmon with red pepper sauce

Sauce

- 1 tablespoon olive oil
- 1 onion, finely chopped
- 2 sticks celery, finely chopped
- 1 tin red peppers without seeds (Pimentos del piquillo)
- 1 dessertspoon smoked sweet paprika
- 1 dessertspoon ground cumin
- 1 dessertspoon tomato purée
- 1 dessertspoon white sugar
- 500ml vegetable or fish stock
- Salt and pepper
- Tabasco sauce for a bit of a kick!

Salmon

- Oil to fry
- 160g salmon per person
- 1 tablespoon paprika
- 1 tablespoon plain flour
- Salt and pepper

Sauce

1 Sweat the onion and celery in the oil until soft.
2 Add the red pepper, cumin, paprika, and salt and pepper. Cook for a few minutes.
3 Add the purée and mix well.
4 Add the stock and sugar and simmer for 10–15 minutes.
5 Blend the mixture in a food processor until smooth.

Salmon

1 Cut the salmon into thin slices.
2 Place the flour, paprika and the salt and pepper in a bowl.
3 Coat each piece of salmon in the flour mixture to cover them completely.
4 Heat a little oil in the frying pan and fry the pieces for a few minutes on each side.
5 Serve with the sauce.

Wine Recommendation
This is a fish dish with a touch of spice so try a white wine with some body, such as a Domaine Ogereau's Chenin Blanc from the Loire. Or a Southern French rosé would be good.

60   6

- 1 dessertspoon oil
- 1 small onion
- ½ red pepper and ½ yellow pepper
- 1 small courgette
- 60g mushrooms
- 1 stick celery
- 1 carrot
- 1 small tin of red kidney beans
- 50g breadcrumbs
- 1 teaspoon vegetable stock powder
- ¼ teaspoon caraway seeds
- ½ teaspoon mixed herbs
- Salt and pepper
- Egg wash
- Plain flour in a bowl, seasoned
- 150 g sunflower seeds
- Oil

Sauce
- 1 dessertspoon oil
- 250g red onions, thinly sliced
- 1 dessertspoon tomato purée
- 1 dessertspoon plain flour
- 200ml red wine
- 150ml vegetable stock
- 2 teaspoons Worcester sauce
- ½ teaspoon thyme
- ½ teaspoon brown sugar
- Salt and pepper

Sunflower seed patties with red onion sauce

The sunflower seeds make for really tasty patties and this is a very healthy meal. Make the sauce in advance and it is possible to store the little patties in the fridge before cooking.

1. Dice all the vegetables finely.
2. Heat the oil in a pan and sweat the vegetables until soft.
3. Drain the water from the red kidney beans and blend them in a food processor. Add a little water if necessary.
4. Add half the vegetables to the kidney beans and blend again. There is no need for these to be totally smooth.
5. Place the mixture from the processor in a bowl with the remainder of the vegetables, breadcrumbs, stock, caraway seeds and the herbs and seasoning.
6. Leave the mixture to chill before making the patties.
7. To make the patties, take a dessertspoon of the mixture and form a ball. Carefully, because it can be quite difficult to shape, roll the ball in flour and flatten to make a patty shape, then dip into the egg wash. Be ready to get your hands dirty!
8. Cover the patties with the sunflower seeds and place on a plate ready to fry.
9. Heat the oil in the pan over a medium heat, and cook the patties for about five minutes on each side until the sunflower seeds are nicely browned.

Sauce
1. Fry the onions in the oil and leave them to brown a little to give the sauce flavour.
2. Add the purée and flour and mix well.
3. Add the wine and stock, a little at a time, in order that it thickens.
4. Add the remainder of the ingredients and cook for about 15 minutes.

60   4

Almond and vegetable baskets

Baskets
- 1 packet of filo pastry
- Melted butter

Small ovenproof pudding bowls about 15 cm in diameter to shape the pastry

Gas mark 5/190°C

Filling
- 25g butter
- 250g mixed vegetables (e.g. onion, celery, pepper, carrots)
- 250g mixed vegetables ready cooked (e.g. cauliflower, broccoli, French beans, peas, sweetcorn)
- 125ml white wine
- 125ml vegetable stock
- 125ml double cream
- ½ teaspoon mixed herbs
- 1 teaspoon cornflour mixed with a little cold water
- Salt and pepper
- 120g whole almonds, roasted until light brown

This was my lovely late mother in law Mari's favourite dish in the restaurant. I thought a farmer's wife choosing the vegetarian option from the menu was quite an achievement!

Baskets
1. Cut the filo pastry into squares 25cm x 25cm. You will need three pieces for each basket.
2. Place one piece of the pastry on a clean surface and brush with melted butter.
3. Place the other piece of pastry on top of the first but slightly angled. Brush with melted butter again.
4. Finally place the third square of pastry on top of the other two, again, slightly angled. Now it should look like a star shape. Brush with melted butter.
5. Carefully, with a palette knife, lift the star and turn over an ovenproof bowl (the butter side should be next to the bowl). This should fold naturally over the sides of the bowl. The edges should be about the same level around the bowl so that it forms a symmetrical basket after cooking.
6. Place the bowls with the baskets over them on a baking tray and bake for 15–20 minutes until they are brown and crisp.
7. Remove from the oven and take the pastry off the ceramic bowls. Leave to cool on a rack.
8. These can be stored for a week or so in a plastic tub. Reheat them in the oven when you want to fill and serve them.

Filling

1 Melt the butter in a saucepan and sweat off the vegetables that are not already cooked, until they are soft.

2 Add the wine and stock and boil until it has reduced to half.

3 Add the cream, the herbs and seasoning and bring back to the boil.

4 Mix the cornflour with a little cold water and add to the mixture, mix well to thicken.

5 Add the remainder of the cooked vegetables to heat. It is important not to overcook.

6 Just before serving, stir in the almonds.

7 Give each person a basket on the plate and fill with the vegetable mixture. Garnish with chopped parsley.

60   4

Spinach and spring onion roulade with tomato, orange and ginger sauce

Roulade
- 300g washed spinach
- 5 eggs, separated
- 50g Gruyere cheese
- 50g Parmesan cheese
- 150ml double cream
- Pinch of nutmeg
- 1 teaspoon vegetable stock powder
- Salt and pepper

Gas mark 6 / 200°

Swiss roll tin 25cm x 33cm, lined with greaseproof paper
Extra greaseproof paper for making the roulade

Filling
- 25g butter
- 2 bunches spring onions, quite finely chopped
- 400g soft cheese, such as Philadelphia
- ½ tsp ground cumin
- ½ tsp vegetable stock powder
- Salt and pepper

Often, vegetarians feel they are paid lip-service in restaurants. This dish is striking to look at and tastes good. You can make it in advance and keep it in the fridge. Serve as a starter or main course.

Roulade
1 Cook the spinach in the microwave for 3 minutes. You can use a bowl or cook it in the packet if it's ready washed, just pierce the bag. Leave to chill and squeeze out the water.
2 Put the spinach in the processor with the egg yolks, cheese, cream, nutmeg, stock powder and seasoning. Process until it is quite smooth.
3 Whisk the egg white until they form stiff peaks.
4 Add the spinach mixture to the egg whites and fold in gently with a large metal spoon, taking care to keep the air in.
5 Spread this onto the tin, already lined with greaseproof paper.
6 Bake for 15–20 minutes until it is firm to the touch when you press with your finger.
7 Put a fresh piece of greaseproof paper on a worktop and carefully turn the spinach sponge onto it, making sure it doesn't break. Leave to cool before removing the greaseproof paper.

Filling
1 Melt the butter in a saucepan and sweat the onions until they are soft.
2 Remove the saucepan from the heat and mix in the cream cheese and the remainder of the ingredients. Mix well.
3 Leave to cool.
4 Spread the mixture onto the spinach sponge.

5   Next, you need to roll it as you would a swiss roll. Using the greaseproof paper that remains underneath it, lift the long side of the sponge. It will begin to roll in on itself. As you keep lifting the paper, it will form the shape of the roulade. Keep doing this until it has formed a long sausage shape with the greaseproof paper still on the outside to keep the shape.

6   Twist the paper at both ends and place in the fridge to cool.

Sauce

1   Place the oil in a saucepan and sweat the onion and celery until soft.

2   Add the remainder of the ingredients except for the ginger and simmer for 15–20 minutes.

3   Blend the mixture in a processor until fairly smooth.

4   Add the ginger and a little of the syrup.

5   To serve, slice portions of the roulade and reheat, then pour over the hot sauce.

Sauce

- 1 dessertspoon olive oil
- 1 onion, finely chopped
- 2 sticks celery, finely chopped
- 1 dessertspoon tomato purée
- 1 400g tin chopped tomatoes
- 1 orange, zest and juice
- 1 dessertspoon sugar
- 1 piece stem ginger, finely chopped
- 1 teaspoon vegetable stock powder
- Salt and pepper

Austria

I like going to Austria. The people are friendly and run very efficient businesses.

A school skiing trip to Austria did not particularly appeal to my wife but she brought home some gifts that were my introduction to the quality of Austrian wine. We don't see much wine from this country in Britain these days because of the wine 'scandal' of nearly 30 years ago, when a few companies had contaminated wine with diethylene glycol (NOT anti-freeze as was hysterically reported in the press at the time). Britain had been importing over 1 million litres every year before this but this dropped to below 100,000 litres. These days, we import about 250,000 litres.

However, this cloud brought its own brand of silver lining and Austria progressed from a country producing medium-sweet wines with the price governing the quality, to the production of top quality sweet and dry wines and even reds too. These are well worth exploring in my opinion and offer a refreshing change with grapes such as Grüner Veltliner or Blaufränkisch, and the sweet wines are absolutely delicious.

The perils of growing grapes

Fortunately for me, the Austrians are often fluent speakers of English. I have a smattering of Spanish and French but my German is non-existent! I regularly buy from Kirnbauer in Burgenland, less than two miles from the border with Hungary. These vineyards are also very close to the huge lake Neusiedler See and it is an important site on the migratory route of birds. Unfortunately, the birds are as skilled as the winemaker when judging the ripeness of grapes and when they are ready to harvest. One year, Marcus Kirnbauer lost his whole crop of Chardonnay in two hours to a flock of hungry starlings when the grapes were just ready to be picked!

Eiswein

In the Neusiedler See region they specialise in the production of sweet wines. These are made from very mature grapes that are affected by botrytis (noble rot) and some use the very special techniques to make Eiswein. To make Eiswein, you need to leave the grapes on the vine throughout the autumn and then harvest them in the early morning while the temperature is at least -7°C. They will need to rise very early, about 4am, and harvest in the tractor light whilst the water in the grape is frozen. They then press them immediately to extract the sweet syrup to make the wine.

This is a very sweet wine but, like all good dessert wines, there is a counter balance of acidity. It is not possible to make wines every year because some years the grapes will rot before they have an opportunity to harvest – or if the birds eat them!

The Welschriesling grape is used here and could cause confusion, but there is absolutely no connection between Wales and the grape, nor is the grape related to the more familiar German Riesling.

Chocolate slice

20   8

- 225g Nice biscuits, crushed
- 120g mixed nuts, finely chopped
- 65g glacé cherries, finely chopped
- 225g dried mixed fruit
- 225g dark chocolate
- 175g butter
- 85g caster sugar
- 2 eggs
- 4 dessertspoons sherry and cognac

Bread tin, lined with greaseproof paper

This is a very rich pudding. There is no need to cook it and it stores well in the fridge.

1 Mix the biscuits, nuts, cherries and fruit together.
2 Melt the chocolate and butter in the microwave.
3 Mix the butter into the chocolate.
4 Add the eggs and beat in well.
5 Pour the sherry and a cognac into the chocolate mixture.
6 Add the ingredients from step 1 to the chocolate mixture and mix thoroughly.
7 Pour into the bread tin and place in the fridge to chill and set.

30   8

Chocolate tart

Chocolate pastry
- 140g softened butter
- 60g caster sugar
- 1 egg
- Drop of vanilla essence
- 15g cocoa powder
- 220g plain flour

Loose-based tin

Gas mark 4/180°C

Filling
- 450g dark chocolate
- 120g butter
- 350ml double cream
- 40g caster sugar
- Zest of ½ an orange
- ½ teaspoon vanilla essence
- 150ml milk

Chocolate pastry
1 Mix the butter and sugar until it is smooth.
2 Add the egg and vanilla and mix well.
3 Sieve the flour and cocoa powder into the mixture.
4 Form a ball using a little of the flour to stop it sticking.
5 Place in the fridge wrapped in cling film for half an hour.
6 Roll out the pastry to a thickness of 1cm or thinner.
7 Line the tin with the pastry and, with a fork, prick the bottom of the pastry before baking blind (cooking the pastry before putting the filling in it). Cover the pastry with greaseproof paper and fill with ceramic or dried peas. This will ensure that the pastry remains flat.
8 Cook for about 20 minutes.

Filling
1 Melt the chocolate and butter in the microwave, stirring occasionally.
2 In a saucepan, bring the double cream, sugar, orange and vanilla to the boil.
3 Pour this mixture onto the melted chocolate and mix well.
4 Mix in the cold milk.
5 Pour into the pastry case.
6 Place in the fridge to set and serve with double cream.

30   6

Chocolate and Amaretto mousse

- 1 (5g) gelatin leaf, soaked in cold water for 5 minutes to soften
- 150g dark chocolate
- 2 eggs, separated
- 40g caster sugar
- 35ml Amaretto
- 150ml double cream
- 40g Amaretti biscuits, crushed

6 ramekins with the crushed biscuits placed in the bottom. (You can also pour a little Amaretto over the biscuits if you wish).

1 Melt the chocolate in a large bowl in the microwave.
2 Mix the egg yolk and the Amaretto into the chocolate.
3 Remove the gelatin from the cold water and place in a saucepan. Dissolve the gelatin with a little cold water so that it doesn't stick (no more than about a teaspoon of cold water).
4 Mix the dissolved gelatin into the chocolate.
5 Beat the egg white with the caster sugar until stiff.
6 In another bowl, whip the cream until it forms soft peaks.
7 It is important that the chocolate is not too warm because it will melt the cream, but do not let it set either.
8 Carefully, fold the cream into the chocolate.
9 Finally, fold the egg whites into the mixture and divide all of it between the six ramekins, with the biscuits on the bottom.
10 Place in the fridge to chill and set.

30   8

White chocolate cheesecake

- 225g digestive biscuits, finely crushed
- 60g butter, melted
- 300g soft cheese such as Philadelphia
- 150g caster sugar
- 1 teaspoon vanilla essence
- 225g white chocolate, melted
- 300ml double cream

Loose-based tin lined with cling film

1 Mix the melted butter and the biscuits well and cover the bottom of the tin. Press down with the back of a spoon to create a solid and even base.
2 With a hand whisk, mix the cheese, sugar and vanilla until smooth.
3 Add the melted white chocolate into the mixture.
4 Whip the cream until soft and fold into the mixture.
5 Pour the mixture over the biscuit base in the tin and smooth with a palette knife.
6 Place in the fridge to set.

Wine Recommendation
It is very difficult to match chocolate and wine because it is such a strong flavour. The wine has to be very powerful and sweet. A fortified wine is best in my opinion such as Madeira, Marsala or even a Tawny Port. Quite a bit of this style of wine is made in Australia and it's worth experimenting with one such as Rutherglen.

30   6

Passionfruit and mango mousse

- 3 eggs, separated
- 125g caster sugar
- 175ml passionfruit and mango smoothie
- 2 gelatin leaves soaked in a little cold water to soften
- 150ml double cream

6 large wine glasses

It is easy to make this mousse with the variety of smoothies that are so popular these days.

1 Whisk the 3 egg yolks and sugar to form a smooth, creamy and thick mixture.
2 Mix in the smoothie.
3 Place the mixture in a saucepan and heat gently. You must keep stirring the mixture as it thickens.
4 Remove from heat. Remove the gelatin leaves from the water and squeeze the excess water out of them and add them to the mixture, stirring well.
5 Leave to cool.
6 Whisk the cream to form soft peaks.
7 Carefully, ensuring that the mixture in the saucepan has chilled, fold in the double cream.
8 Whisk the 3 egg whites and fold into the mixture.
9 Divide the mixture into the individual glasses and place in the fridge to set.

For variety, you can place fruit and sponge in the bottom of the glasses and add smoothie before putting the mousse on top.

50   8

Apricot and orange tart

Sweet pastry

- 140g softened butter
- 60g caster sugar
- 1 egg
- Drop of almond essence
- 225g plain flour

Loose-based flan tin

Gas mark 4/180°C

Filling

- 150g apricots
- 5 eggs
- 150g caster sugar
- 400ml double cream
- ½ teaspoon almond essence
- 1 orange, zest and juice

Sweet pastry

1 Mix the butter and sugar until smooth.
2 Add the egg and the almond essence and mix again.
3 Sift the flour into the mixture and mix well.
4 Form a ball with the pastry and use a little extra flour to prevent the dough sticking.
5 Place in the fridge wrapped in cling film for half an hour.
6 Roll out the pastry with plenty of flour to stop it sticking, to about 1cm thick, or thinner if possible.
7 Line the tin with the pastry and, with a fork, prick the base of the pastry before baking it blind. Cover the pastry with greaseproof paper and fill with ceramic or dried peas.
8 Cook for about 30 minutes.

Filling

1 Chop the apricots into quarters and place in a bowl with a zest and the juice. Cook in the microwave for about a minute and leave to soak until cold.
2 Beat the eggs and sugar together well.
3 Add the cream and any juice that has not been soaked into the apricots to the egg and sugar mixture.
4 Place the apricots in the bottom of the pastry case and pour the mixture over them.
5 Bake for about 30 minutes until the middle has set.

20   8

Almond and orange sponge

- 225g butter
- 1 teaspoon almond essence
- 225g caster sugar
- 4 eggs
- 275g self raising flour, sifted
- 75g ground almonds
- 1 orange, zest and juice
- 1 orange, segmented and finely chopped

Bread tin lined with greaseproof paper

Gas mark 4/180°C

1 Mix the butter, almond essence and sugar until the mixture is thick and creamy.
2 Add the eggs, one at a time, mixing thoroughly before adding each one.
3 Add the flour, ground almonds and orange zest and mix well.
4 Add the juice and then the orange segments. If the mixture is a little too thick, add a dessertspoon of milk to loosen it a bit.
5 Place the mixture in the bread tin and cover with foil.
6 Place the tin in a roasting tin and pour hot water to reach halfway up the bread tin. Cover it all with foil to create a bain-marie.
7 Bake for one hour. Test to make sure it is cooked in the middle by piercing with a skewer, which should be clean on removal.

This is delicious with custard, and adding a dessertspoon of orange marmalade gives it an extra dimension.

Wine Recommendation
A traditional Sauternes would work well, made from botrytized grapes, with aromas and flavours of orange peel and marmalade.

20   8

Meringues and Port-poached fruit

Meringues
- 4 egg whites
- 225g caster sugar

Oven on the lowest
temperature
Baking tray lined with
greaseproof paper

Fruit
- 400ml Port
- 500g sugar
- 2 cinnamon sticks
- 1kg berry fruits – fresh
  or frozen
- 1 tablespoon cornflour

My meringue recipe is very simple with just egg whites and sugar. Often I will make them and leave them in the oven overnight on the lowest possible temperature to obtain a lovely crunchy texture. They keep in a sealed plastic tub for a considerable time.

Meringues
1 Whisk the 4 egg whites until they begin to form a thick mixture.
2 Add the sugar, a spoonful at a time, continuously whisking. Continue to whisk until the meringue is thick and shiny.
3 Fill a piping bag with the mixture and pipe the shapes onto the baking tray. Keep them consistent in size.
4 Place on the bottom shelf of the oven for several hours (as least 4) until they are crisp.
5 Serve with the fruit and whisked double cream.

Poached fruit
1 Bring the Port, sugar and cinnamon to the boil and simmer until sugar has dissolved.
2 Add the fruit and bring the entire mixture to the boil.
3 Mix the cornflour in a cup with a little cold water and add this to the hot fruit, stirring in to thicken.
4 Remove from the heat and leave to cool. You can store this in the fridge for some time.

20   8

Elderflower and raspberry jelly

Jelly
- 7 gelatin leaves (5g each)
- 175ml elderflower cordial
- 625ml of water
- 75g sugar
- 300g raspberries

Sauce
- 300g raspberries
- 50g sugar
- ¼ lemon – zest and juice

Terrine or bread tin
22cm x 12cm x 7cm

This takes time to construct the different layers but it is a very striking and pretty pudding.

Jelly
1 Place the gelatin leaves to soak in plenty of cold water to cover them for some minutes until they are soft.
2 Heat the water, cordial and sugar until dissolved.
3 Remove the gelatin leaves from the cold water and stir them into the warm mixture.
4 Leave to cool in the saucepan. Do not allow to set.
5 Line the tin with cling film. Pour 1cm of the jelly in the bottom of the tin and place in the fridge to set.
6 When it has set, arrange half of the raspberries on the jelly and then pour enough additional jelly to cover them. Return to the fridge to set again.
7 Repeat a further two times to construct the layers.
8 When you are ready to serve, turn the jelly out onto a plate. Warm a knife in hot water to cut neat slices, and serve with the sauce and cream.

Sauce
1 To make a simple sauce, place the fruits in a processor with the sugar and lemon and process until smooth.
2 Finally, push the sauce through a sieve to get rid of any seeds and store in the fridge.

Wine Recommendation
Fruity desserts go well with light, frothy, sweet sparkling wines. Asti may have a bad reputation but this is where it can come into its own. We import a superb French equivalent, Clairette de Die, or look out for Moscato. These tend to be light in alcohol and are perfect to enjoy on a sunny afternoon in the garden with a few strawberries.

30   6

Banana Éclairs

Choux Buns
(See wild garlic choux buns in the Canapés and Tapas chapter)

- 2 bananas
- 60g brown sugar
- 1 teaspoon lemon juice
- ¼ teaspoon ground cinnamon
- 350ml double cream
- Maple syrup
- Icing sugar

Gas mark 6 / 200°C

1 Follow the recipe for choux buttons on p 50. Instead of piping little buns, pipe long lines like thin sausages.
2 Bake in the same way as the wild garlic buns for 20–30 minutes until they are crisp on the outside.
3 Mash the bananas into a pulp with the lemon, sugar and cinnamon.
4 Whisk the cream until it forms soft peaks.
5 Add the banana mixture to the cream and fold in with a large spoon until it is thoroughly mixed.
6 Slice the éclairs in half, pipe the mixture into the middle and puts the top back on.
7 Drizzle some of the maple syrup over the éclairs and sprinkle icing sugar over them to serve.

Wine Recommendation
If you would like dessert wine with this, try something that has tropical fruits to go with the banana, and that is sweet enough to balance the syrup. Chile is turning out some excellent examples these days, such as the Valdivieso Eclat Semillon.

20   8

Cointreau ice cream

- 225g caster sugar
- 5 eggs
- 5 egg yolks
- Fine zest of 1 orange
- 35ml Cointreau
- 600ml double cream

This ice cream is very simple and easy to adapt and experiment with different flavours. Remember to remove from the freezer 5–10 minutes before serving in order to soften it. You will have egg whites left over, so you can use these to make meringues.

1 Beat the eggs with the sugar for about 5 minutes until they form a thick, smooth and creamy mixture.
2 Add the zest and Cointreau.
3 Whisk the cream until it is soft and fold into the mixture.
4 Pour into a plastic tub and freeze.
5 Serve with segments of fresh orange.

Alcohol in ice cream means it will not freeze as solidly and will be easier to serve.

30   8

Praline ice cream

Praline

- 150g caster sugar
- 150g whole almonds

Well-greased baking tray

Ice cream

- 225g caster sugar
- 5 eggs
- 5 egg yolks
- 1 teaspoon almond essence
- 600ml double cream

Praline

1 Place the sugar and nuts in a heavy saucepan on a low heat. But keep a close eye on it, stirring occasionally, because it can easily burn.
2 When the sugar has dissolved and has a caramel colour to it, pour onto the baking tray very carefully because it will be extremely hot. Leave to cool.
3 Now you can have fun smashing the praline. Break into small pieces – you can use a rolling pin on a suitable surface – again, carefully!
4 This will store for a while in a plastic bag if you squeeze all of the air out of it.

Ice cream

1 Beat the eggs together with the sugar for about 5 minutes until it is thick, smooth and creamy.
2 Add the almond essence.
3 Whisk the cream until it is soft and then fold into the mixture.
4 Fold in 3–4 tablespoons of the praline.
5 Pour into a plastic tub and place in the freezer.
6 After about an hour and a half, remove from the freezer and mix again, so that the praline does not sink to the bottom.

Portugal

We honeymooned in Portugal, but it was a long time before I returned there on the wine trail. It's surprising, really, because the country produces one of the best fortified wines in the world: Port. On that early holiday we went to Setúbal, where they make a sweet wine. This was our first visit to a vineyard after opening Dylanwad Da in 1988 and we went out of pure curiosity – we had no thoughts of importing back then. One thought did strike me, though: why here? A small peninsula below Lisbon – why was this spot unique?

PORTUGAL

The name 'Port' is derived from the city of Oporto where, traditionally, all the wines from the region upstream were sent to be matured. It's the sort of place I love: a working city that hasn't been over-sanitised. If you go to Oporto (and I would advise anyone to do so), walk down the steep little streets to the river and you'll catch a glimpse every so often of the famous port lodges on the other side of the river at Vila Nova de Gaia. Here the wines mature, and famous brand names adorn the rooflines in huge capital letters. Walk over the iron bridge and take a tour, you'll start to understand what makes these wines so special. This is where, in the old days, the wines arrived on boats brought along the treacherous river from the vineyards up country. You have to travel 50 miles or more upstream to reach the vineyards that produce the grapes for some of these classic wines.

The climate is harsh – dry and extremely hot in the summer but freezing cold and windy in the winter. The best vines are grown on narrow terraces on some impossibly steep slopes. The grapes are handpicked and traditionally put in granite 'lagars' and trodden with (clean I hope!) feet. The reason for some of the best wines still being pressed by foot is to extract the juice carefully, swiftly and gently to start a very quick fermentation. What a far cry from the enormous flat vineyards of places like central California with machine-harvested grapes and computer controls in the winery. Port is different to ordinary still wines because it has been fortified with high alcohol spirit. Unlike sherry, which is fortified after the wine has finished fermenting, with Port, the fermentation is halted by adding alcohol, killing the yeasts and leaving natural sugars in the wine – essentially making a sweet red wine.

Cheese and wine

Port is seen as a natural partner for cheese because of the sweetness but it's possible to forget the wide variety of cheese there is today. A fresh goat's cheese that is soft and acidic could partner well with a Sauvignon. Or a strong hard cheese that we produce so well in Britain is more at home with a red wine with a stronger structure such as Cabernet Sauvignon or a Syrah. Blue cheeses that are sweet and creamy can make a divine match when paired with a sweet wine such as Sauternes or a sweet and nutty old Tawny Port. Such are the joys of experimenting and playing with flavours!

A plate of cheese and apple pickle is something that I have enjoyed since I was a little boy. Cheese can be a perfect end to dinner or served as a lunchtime meal with bread and pickle. Indeed, our default choice of food if we want to have friends over for a chat is to offer a plate of cheese to enjoy together and the selection of Welsh cheeses available now, from feta and goat's cheese to hard and blue cheese is absolutely delicious. Make it special with a large bowl of fruit or fresh figs. Llinos likes to roast tomatoes with herbs, olive oil and balsamic for a lovely bread-dipping dish to go with it. Membrillo, the sweet Spanish quince paste, is another accompaniment that is now more widely available that I would opt for. This can be a real feast, my mouth is watering just writing about it. Choose good quality artisan bread or a variety of biscuits in a basket. You can justify buying a bottle of Marsala or a good sherry if there's a crowd of you and you can compare the taste with the different flavours of cheese. Enjoy!

White Port makes an excellent aperitif.

163

Wines from unexpected regions

WALES

It took me a few years to discover a good Welsh wine to sell in the restaurant. Luckily, I discovered Ancre Hill in Monmouth when organising a staff outing to an English vineyard, Three Choirs, that is not so far away over the border. Richard Morris of Ancre Hill Estates planted his first vines in 2006. Richard professes to a life-long love of wine and, although a Chartered Accountant by trade, he had always dreamt of producing his own wine. When he first embarked on making this dream a reality, his attentions were fixed on overseas sites, travelling as far as Tasmania and Central Otago. It was not until he attended a course in Plumpton College that he realised that his home at Ancre Hill potentially had all that was necessary to make a top quality wine. The south-facing slopes enjoy long sunshine hours and are well sheltered by tree-topped hills to the north and south. The nearby Brecon Beacons also provide shelter from rain, resulting in a much lower average rainfall than the rest of the country.

The site's history may also provide further evidence of its suitability, Ancre Hill having been built in the 17th century by French Huguenots: a group famous for planting vines in their settlements. Richard suspects that the Huguenots chose Ancre Hill because of its prime growing conditions and the abundant water supply from the natural springs beneath the old Welsh longhouse.

This one man's epiphany led him to embark upon further research, instructing Newcastle University to analyse samples of the site's limestone soil and carefully studying Met Office records to assess the suitability of the climate. His findings were encouraging and he therefore proceeded to tackle the next dilemma – grape selection. The initial plantings consisted of three varieties: Seyval Blanc, Triomphe and later, Pinot Noir. Success soon followed, with the first vintage's sparkling wine being awarded a silver medal in the *Decanter* magazine wine awards. However, the low sugar content in the Seyval Blanc meant that chaptalisation was inevitable; the maximum permitted 3% alcohol increase being required.

They then faced a dilemma – whether to keep the Seyval Blanc. This led to the brave decision to grub up half of the Seyval vines in April 2007 to replace them with Albarino, a grape he believed is well-suited to Ancre Hill's unique growing environment, and not just because of its ability to tolerate wet weather. Having researched the variety's growth in the vineyards of Galicia, he noted that his rainfall levels were half of that experienced in these vineyards and that, although the Galicians enjoyed warmer summers, the two climates shared many similarities.

One of the markers of their success was the winning of a competition in Italy, triumphing over sparkling wines from all over the world and Champagne – including Bollinger! This is not so surprising when we look at the geography and consider that South-East Wales is on more or less the same latitude as Champagne in Northern France and shares the same type of rock and climate.

Other promising vineyards in Wales are further north than I would have imagined possible: Penygroes near Caernarfon sees Pant Du producing wine, as well as delicious ciders and apple juice. Llaethliw vineyard just south of Aberystwyth has an equally enthusiastic and dedicated family, growing grapes to produce a quality wine. Vines take a while to mature but what a pleasure it is to see adventurous individuals like this showing such passion and commitment to their projects, firmly believing that there is a place for Welsh wine on the market amongst other Welsh produce such as meat and cheese. And I have to say, I totally agree.

Some of the best Welsh and English sparkling wines compete favourably with Champagne.

ARMENIA

Occasionally, I take a trip to London to the huge commercial wine fairs in search of something different. It's difficult for individuals to stand out amongst hundreds of other producers and sellers. However, one man from Armenia with a single wine on his stand caught my attention immediately. He threw me instantly with his response to where I was from: 'Wales! We know Wales in Armenia. Small country, lots of mountains, not many people!' Within seconds I was mentally planning my journey to this fascinating country. That night, after arriving home, I was to be found in the living room: atlas on my lap and an Internet search for a flight to Yerevan.

Recent discoveries of wine-making equipment in a cave, dating back more than 6,000 years, mean that this small country can lay claim to being one of the earliest wine producing countries. The prospects of this trip were exciting. I emailed Zorah, the producer, and a reply stated that spring would be a pleasant time of year to visit or possibly the autumn, when the local wine fair took place. I replied that my options were limited as a restaurateur – that is, February. I could almost hear the 'Ah!' of worry emanating out of the email that stated 'You are likely to have snow' and I did. With my wife's warnings in my ear about not venturing near the border with neighbouring Iran, I set off on my first journey to this interesting country in 2012.

There is only one road leading south in Armenia and in my tiny hire car I followed huge tankers the whole way to the border of Iran to find electric fences, apparently still in use. I never did work out who they were intending to keep in or out of which country. On my return journey north, I turned onto a muddy track that led to the village where Zorah is produced. This is a one shop, one church sort of place and I went to the shop to enquire about the way to the vineyard. No-one spoke any English (nor Welsh!) and after about quarter of an hour of trying to communicate, with pictures of grapes drawn and a photo of the wine label, a small crowd had gathered around me and my little car – people shouting into their mobile phones. Eventually, a jovial, rotund man arrived in his beaten-up Lada to guide me to the vineyard. I followed him out of the village and over a muddy field. I was surprised to see he was a sort of 'guardian' of the vineyard and was living in an old metal shipping container with his dogs. There was a splendid view of the vines disappearing into the distance but I only saw the foundations of the winery. It was yet to be built. Neither did I see where the wine was produced, but I was fascinated to learn that some of the wine is aged in clay amphorae, just like the ones used 6,000 years ago. A year later, visiting a biodynamic vineyard in Italy, I found myself looking the same type of amphorae lined up in their winery. How fascinating it is to think of this link between countries and across centuries.

It's worth venturing to new horizons because it seems likely by now that there are few places on earth where people are not willing to chance their hand at making wine. In a tasting with the Gellifor Wine Club run by a very knowledgeable friend Alan, we enjoyed tasting wines from Japan and Thailand amongst others. China is developing to be a major producer in the world. It is so interesting to see the developments in the industry and I cannot deny that part of the fascination is following the wine trail. I do hear that Madagascar is now producing wine. My great grandparents who were missionaries are buried there. Now where's that atlas?

HUNGARY AND EASTERN EUROPE

Another wintery trip in the early days when I forced Llinos my wife on a February holiday in subzero conditions was to Bulgaria in 1993. No expense spared, we flew budget airlines and landed at a military airport surrounded by vines and knee-deep in snow. Customs was in a shed that we stumbled across the field to reach, where a disinterested guard stamped our passports without a glance.

One of our stops was the old capital of Bulgaria: Veliko Tarnovo where we ate in the only open restaurant in town. We were not really there for the wine but we couldn't help but laugh out loud when we were served a bottle of red in the most professional manner with the label proudly pronouncing 'Sainsbury's Bulgarian Merlot'! This was in the days when Bulgaria was still supplying some exceptionally good value wines. They had arrived on the British market in the 1970s, but as the former Soviet Union fell apart, the newly "independent" Bulgaria ran out of money to buy equipment and barrels and even, sadly, fuel for their tractors at the collectivised vineyards, and quality slumped. It has taken a while, but it looks like the wine industry there is on its way up again I'm glad to say.

More recently, I had the opportunity to travel to Hungary, a country that produces cheap wine of a high standard in the Lake Balaton region. I'm sure everyone of a certain age remembers Bull's Blood! However, this was not why I was there, I was in search of one of the world's finest and oldest sweet wines: Tokay. So special, it was said that Catherine the Great had a group of hussars for the single purpose of transferring this wine from Hungary to the court in St Petersburg.

One of the first to spot the potential in the world market for reinstating this classic wine after the fall of the Iron Curtain was Hugh Johnson. He searched for the magical and famous wines and helped to bring them back to the wine drinkers of the world. Thanks to his help and contacts, I was now bouncing around one of these unique Royal Tokaji Wine Company vineyards near Mád, in an old Russian jeep.

Following this, we had a tour of the cellars, seemingly miles of tunnels underground that were jam-packed with the ageing wines. Rooted in my memory is what looked like an old builder's skip, full of raisined grapes, hand-picked one by one to make this delicious wine. This is what creates the incredible sweetness in the wine and the most valuable is Essencia; this is made with the "free-run" juice of these raisins. It can take decades to ferment because they are so packed with sugar. I once bought a few little 'Alice in Wonderland' bottles – just 10cl, but at a cost of more than £20 a bottle!

I have started importing from Moldova too. There is huge potential in Eastern Europe, with excellent geographical and geological conditions in countries such as Georgia and Romania. I can't wait to expand the range on my shelves in the shop!

Menu suggestions

When I used to plan menus I would look carefully at the balance. Vegetarians will look for protein in their meals, so you have to include pulses, nuts or cheese in one of the courses. I try not to put cream in every single meal and this is worth considering when you prepare your own menus. My wife notices immediately if ingredients crop up more than once over different courses, so I would always ask her to cast an eye, not only at my spelling but also to check that there is a good balance to the meal..

A Tapas Party

Salmon and lime pinwheels
Wild garlic choux buns
Fina's Tortilla
Mini Welsh lamb burgers
Olives
Nuts

A Tapas party for a warm day. There is a balance of fish, meat and vegetarian tapas here and not too much cheese or cream with a range of different flavours from the lime to the mint in the burgers giving structure to the meal. You can put the tortilla on a slice of French bread and this makes the food go further. Drink a wine from Spain with this, maybe a Verdejo from Rueda.

A Feast, with a wine to match each course

Canapés – Ancre Hill sparkling
Chicken and ham terrine – Sauvignon
Pen Llŷn crab chowder – Riesling
Riojan lamb – Rioja Reserva
Apricot and orange tart – Sauternes
Cheese – Tawny Port

Whilst I was slaving away on many a New Year's Eve, my family decided that they would replicate the meal that was being served in the restaurant at home with a wine to match every course. This is fun to do – divide the work by allocating a course and matching wine to members of the family to prepare.

Choose light canapés such as the pinwheels or the chorizo lollipops and possibly a bowl of olives. The chowder is very creamy so use a sharp sauce with the Chicken and ham terrine, such as Cumberland sauce. The dark sauce with the lamb is a good contrast before the pudding..

A Picnic

For years now it has been a little tradition to take our staff for a picnic. As well as sandwiches, it's nice to have something different to share. Of course, it's important to ensure that the food is easy to eat with your hands. I include a little pot of apple chutney for everyone to use as a dip. Maybe a fish pasty sounds a little odd but truly they are very tasty cold. Our son Mei used to enjoy one of these in his lunchbox when they were on the menu in the restaurant.

Glamorgan sausages
Faggot
Chicken and apple turnover
Salmon and prawn pasty
Cherry tomatoes
Cucumber, cut into batons
2 small plastic tubs: one chutney/one mayonnaise
Squares of chocolate slice
Tub of strawberries

A Romantic Meal for Two

This is a light meal, with beautiful colours in the salad as a starter. It isn't difficult to cook. Make a Bellini with Prosecco – the remainder will be perfect to drink with the first course. A bottle of Vouvray (or a half bottle maybe!) would be a perfect partner for the chicken.

Bellini as an aperitif
Sugarsnap peas, orange and cucumber salad
Chicken with leek and Pernod sauce
Chocolate and Amaretto mousse

Suppliers

Here is a list of the suppliers of food and drink mentioned in the book.

Cwrw Llŷn
Gweithdai Nefyn, Ffordd Dewi Sant, Nefyn, Pwllheli, Gwynedd LL53 6EG
Tel.: 01758 750243
www.cwrwllyn.com

Yr Ardd Fadarch / The Mushroom Garden
Glan Meirion, Nantmor LL55 4YG
Tel.: 01766 890353
www.snowdoniamushrooms.co.uk

Selective Seafoods
(Gareth Griffiths and Mary White)
Ffridd Wen, Tudweiliog, Pwllheli, Gwynedd LL53 8BJ
Tel.: 01758 770397
www.selectiveseafoods.com

T. J. Roberts a'i Fab (Butcher)
Stryd Fawr, Y Bala
Tel.: 01658 520471
www.welshqualitymeat.co.uk

Roberts Brothers (Butcher)
Y Sgwâr, Dolgellau, Gwynedd LL40 1PY
Tel.: 01341 422619

Ultracomida (Welsh and Spanish produce)
31 Pier Street, Aberystwyth SY23 2LN
Tel.: 01970 630 686
www.ultracomida.co.uk

Popty'r Dref (Bakery)
Ffos y Felin, Dolgellau, Gwynedd LL40 1ET
Tel.: 01341 422507

Pant Du (Vineyard)
Ffordd y Sir, Penygroes, Caernarfon, Gwynedd LL54 6HE
Tel.: 01286 880806 / 875053
www.pantdu.co.uk

Ancre Hill (Vineyard)
Ffordd Rockfield, Trefynwy, Sir Fynwy NP25 5HS
Tel.: 01600 714 152
www.ancrehillestates.co.uk

Aerona Liqueur (Hazel and Gwilym Jones)
Rhedynog Isaf, Chwilog, Pwllheli LL53 6LQ
Tel.: 01766 810387
www.aerona-liqueur.co.uk

Caws Cymru (Richard Harries and Theo Bond)
Uned 1, Wervil Grange, Pentregat, Llandysul, Ceredigion SA44 6HW
Tel.: 01239 654800

Caws Cheddar Organig Hafod (Sam and Rachel Holden)
Holden Farm Dairy, Bwlchwernen Fawr, Llangybi, Llanbedr Pont Steffan SA48 8PS
Tel.: 01570 493 283
www.hafodcheese.co.uk

Llaethliw (Vineyard)
Ciliau Aeron, Lampeter, Ceredigion SA48 7RF
Tel.: 01545 571 879
http://llaethliw.co.uk

Index

Lamb:
  Lamb, Port, plum and ginger pie 102
  Mini Welsh lamb burgers 44
  Riojan lamb 100
  Welsh lamb casserole with Snowdonia
  mushrooms 98
Madeira and mushroom sauce 106
Meringues and Port-poached fruits 150
Mini Welsh lamb burgers 44
Mushrooms:
  Madeira and mushroom sauce 106
  Mushroom pâté 76
  Welsh lamb casserole with Snowdonia
  mushrooms 98
Nuts:
  Almond and orange sponge 148
  Almond and vegetable basket 126
  Chicken with pinenuts and sherry 112
  Chocolate slice 136
  Praline ice cream 158
Paprika salmon with red pepper sauce 122
Passionfruit and mango mousse 144
Pen Llŷn crab chowder 68
Pistou 64
Pork:
  Boston pork and baked beans 110
  Caldo Verde 66
  Chicken and ham terrine 72
  Chorizo lollipops 42
  Faggot 74
  Pork and cranberry pâté 70
Praline ice cream 158
Salmon and prawn pasties 78
Smoked salmon and lime pinwheels 40

Spinach, spring onion roulade with tomato,
orange and ginger sauce 128
Steak with Pommery sauce 104
Sugarsnap peas, orange and cucumber salad 88
Sundried tomato quiche 82
Sunflower seed patties with red onion sauce 124
Tomato:
  Sundried tomato quiche 82
  Spinach and spring onion roulade with
  tomato, orange and ginger sauce 128
  Tomato, goat's cheese and basil tart 84
Vegetables:
  Almond and vegetable basket 126
  Beetroot, goat's cheese and pumpkin seed
  salad 90
  Chicken with leek and Pernod sauce 116
  Chicken with spinach and coconut 114
  Fina's Tortilla 52
  Hake with pea and mint sauce 120
  Mushroom pâté 76
  Pistou 64
  Spinach and spring onion roulade with
  tomato, orange and ginger sauce 128
  Sugarsnap peas, orange and cucumber
  salad 88
  Sundried tomato quiche 82
  Sunflower seed patties with red onion
  sauce 124
  Tomato, goat's cheese and basil tart 84
Welsh lamb casserole with Snowdonia
mushrooms 98
White chocolate cheesecake 142
Wild garlic choux buns 50